MW01125507

IF YOU THINK YOU CAN, YOU CAN

DEFYING EXPECTATIONS

FAMILY, SPORTS & RECREATION

AL "HONDO" HANDY

Defying Expectations

© 2022 Al "Hondo" Handy

ISBN 978-1-66785-291-1

eBook ISBN 978-1-66785-292-8

CONTENTS

DEDICATION

I am honored to dedicate this book to my brother, Ronald Mitchell. Watching Ron's flashy left-handed passes encouraged me to change my style of play on the basketball court. Ronald's quickness and "no-look" passes sometimes surprised teammates. He had a smooth personality that was reflected in the way he carried himself. He wore his shirt collar up rather than down, the style then and now. He inspired me on and off the court. He was always the coolest person I knew. I often wondered what the teachers and the girls in school said about him. Only one girl's opinion really mattered, though. Her name was Peggy, and she eventually became his wife.

Ronald stood far above all the other role models in my life; he stood far above the other role models my friends had. When my life seemed to be spiraling out of control, he pointed me in the right direction. I credit him with saving my life. He accomplished this by sharing only a few words. I called him from a telephone booth to ask for a favor, which I had done several times in the past. He had always come through when I needed money. This time, he listened to me and asked questions, as if he was taking notes. Then he shocked me by saying something that changed my life forever:

Is that all you need?
I answered… *Yes.*

This time he gave me something more valuable than money. He gave me advice.

Here's what I need you to do. Go to your apartment. Get whatever you can take with you. Close your apartment door—and don't look back.

I felt a lump in my throat and the tears began to flow. I was 23 and living in Harford County, Maryland. He encouraged me to pack my bags and go home to start my life over again.

It was the best thing I ever did. I called him to tell him that I made it home. As far as I know, he never shared our conversation with anyone. I guess that's what brothers do. *You can start your life over.* Those words of wisdom have inspired me ever since. He has guided me throughout my entire life. When things aren't going well, I stop to take a deep breath. Then I ask what Ronald would do. Though he's no longer on earth, he still gives me the right answer. When I started this book, I wished he could have been here to help me with it. Then I realized he already had. He gave me the advice to start over.

ACKNOWLEDGMENTS

People who have guided me throughout my life deserve to be acknowledged.

My mother, Lola Handy, always encouraged me to help others, to be kind, thoughtful, and respectful, and not to give up on my dreams.

My Aunt, Sis Radie Fooks, always wrote poems that piqued my interest. I now understand the value of some of her writing.

Ward Lambert, my life mentor and my high school and college basketball coach, continues to motivate me. He once said, *Hondo—if you think you can, you can.* Those words stuck with me and drove me to focus on staying positive throughout my journey.

Gregory Purnell—my confidence mentor, a fantastic speaker, and an inspiring community historian—encouraged me to move forward when things weren't moving fast enough. Greg, thank you for that; I am deeply appreciative.

INTRODUCTION

Bishop is a small town on the Eastern Shore of Maryland. It isn't much bigger than a postage stamp, but it's where I grew up. My mother endured the hardships of the Jim Crow laws: *No drinking from water fountains no using public restrooms. No visiting the inside of a restaurant: only going around the back to get a platter of food.* Life was unfair. Despite this, my mother vowed to push me to be the best I could be. I can still hear her advice. *Don't give up on your dreams to be a better person.*

CHAPTER 1

HOW THE LITTLE ORANGE BALL CHANGED MY LIFE

How could I be successful in sports like my brother Ronald? He played on the hardwood courts at Worcester High School, an all-Black school, before integration. He did everything on the court with a bit of flair. He even looked good when he dribbled and shot basketballs. I wanted to be just like him.

However, before I ever played basketball, I felt a deep affection for running—and I ran everywhere. I used my short stocky legs to move throughout our small community and I don't remember ever being tired. I sprinted to the mailbox, to the store, to my aunts' and uncles' houses. Growing up seemed like a family affair, probably because most of our family lived within half a mile from our home. I would run through the woods to my Aunt Helen's house. I called her HaHa. Even after dark, I would run home as fast as possible. I would hear noises—twigs snapping and the crunch of dried leaves—with every step I made. Feeling like something was behind me made me run faster.

Whenever I visited HaHa, I relished listening to the Baltimore Oriole games on her old radio. I could barely hear the game over the static, but it was better than nothing. My mother didn't own a radio, so listening to HaHa's was a treat. One night, I started home after the Orioles finished playing, and in the dark, I crashed into this big pine tree—a tree that I had always avoided until this time. I guess bad judgment had me glancing away

5

from the path at the wrong moment. It usually took only a few seconds for me to get home from HaHa's. When I didn't make it home that night, my family came looking for me. They found me lying on the ground, knocked out cold. I think something in the woods must have distracted me. I don't really remember. Sixty years later, that tree still stands—thankfully I do, too. Before my 97-year-old Aunt Helen, HaHa, passed in 2019, she reminded me about the tree she always called Albin's tree after my accident there.

Because my older cousins Larry and John (Junie) inspired me, my running distance increased. Larry was an easygoing guy, but he didn't want his younger brother to outdo him in any sport. John was competitive and he was determined to beat Larry. He used every tool he could to accomplish this—whatever it took to win. That's probably why they usually ended up arguing or fighting during their games.

They were too young to drive, so running was their only form of transportation. I chased behind them everywhere they went, so running was my transportation too. They seemed to be jogging, but I was forced to run twice as fast just to keep up. Being six years younger didn't help either. Speeding down the highway, I made sure I kept close to them.

Once we were allowed to play on the school's asphalt courts, we would jump the fence at Phillip C. Showell Elementary School in Selbyville, Delaware after school hours. After hustling up and down the court, shooting baskets, and playing defense for a couple hours, it would be time to head home. Because we used to win, the Delaware guys would chase us away. The two-mile trek home almost became a sprint.

Once I got that little orange ball in my hands, my life changed. I became excited and my entire focus changed. I used to fall asleep with the ball next to me. I did the same with my baseball glove and ball. I remember many wonderful dreams about the game of basketball. I began to dedicate my life to the game. I dribbled while running everywhere I went. I would shoot baskets even when the sun went down. I can still hear my mother calling me:

Albin, it's too dark; it's time to come in!

Still shooting in the dark, I was barely able to see the ball go through the net. But I could hear the net *swishhh*. Having to locate my ball in the dark also meant it was time to go in. My only source of light? One dim light bulb hanging off our back porch.

How many basketballs have I owned? I don't know. It's impossible to remember who gave me my first one. How many shots have I attempted? I don't know. I took shots every chance I got; I even practiced shooting the ball to myself. How many times have I dribbled a basketball? I don't know. I dribbled with one hand behind my back; I dribbled with my eyes closed. What I do know is that without that little orange ball, I would not be where I am today. That basketball fostered a good attitude in me. It was like the ball spoke to me, telling me to always do the right thing. I would do homework and chores after school so I could play ball. I realized that ball made me competitive. It also instilled good sportsmanship: teamwork, respect, responsibility, integrity, perseverance, and fairness were becoming part of me. Some of these positive traits are featured on banners hanging inside Northside Park in Ocean City, Maryland—one of the parks where I worked for many years.

I first fell in love with basketball after watching my uncles play on the weekends. I picked up on different types of shots and fancy and difficult passes. Watching my brother play against basketball players from other schools was amazing. I remember all these people cheering in the stands, jumping up and down when a great play was made.

My dreams of playing on the basketball team started the day I entered high school. I often heard people say that I'd never be able to play basketball because I was simply too short—barely over five feet! From the first time I heard comments like that, I became even more determined. I loved the game that much. I told myself that I would prove them wrong. I realized I could use my quick reflexes and my speed to compete. Years later—during an awards ceremony—my coach shared these words:

Hondo more than made up for his lack of height with his quickness and speed.

That was good enough for me. My confidence went sky high and has never come down. I felt like I could defend anyone on the basketball court. I played every game like a championship game. I realized that playing with heart and speed often led me to overcome an opponent, regardless of his athletic abilities. I understood why hard work could beat talent. I loved challenging the bigger, stronger, taller athletes. I tried to outwork my opponent. I wanted my opponent to think more about me than the game. I wanted my opponent to wonder about me every time he dribbled. I hoped to intercept every pass. Because of my height, I wanted to defy expectations. I think my attitude about success on the basketball court was developed within my family.

In the '60s and '70s, dirt basketball courts sprang up across the country—many times with no nets on the rims. All my friends designed their own courts. There were hundreds of these basketball courts on Maryland's Eastern Shore. Growing up in Bishop, (now Bishopville), we only played on dirt basketball courts. We went in the woods and chopped down a tree. Then we nailed a board to the tree to make a backboard, and then nailed a rim to the backboard—if we were lucky to find a rim. If the rim broke, we used a wooden basket or a milk carton. Digging a hole deep enough for the pole was our next challenge.

You became very popular just by having a dirt basketball court. You were sure to have a backyard full of friends ready to play after school. All the courts started out with grass, but after a few games the grass turned into dirt. We used sticks to mark out the boundaries. Dribbling was the only problem; that was because of an uneven playing surface. Depending on where the ball struck the ground, it could bounce anywhere until it lost air or became flat. The rules would then change: no dribbling, of course—just passing, cutting, and shooting.

Loving the game so much, my friends and I sharpened our skills even in the rain. On windy days in any season, the wind affected our shots—but we would still be out there playing hard. We even shoveled snow off the court to play after winter snowstorms. With freezing hands and fingers, we still competed. Every night throughout at least three seasons, our clothes were covered with mud—and it was caked on our shoes. Kids today wouldn't dare play on dirt courts; they wouldn't want to get their shoes dirty.

We never thought about our mothers having to wash our clothes. With only a washboard to get our clothes clean, the extra laundry kept my mother busy. Later we obtained a hand-me – down washing machine, and this aspect of life became easier for Mom.

In my sophomore summer, my cousin Larry got me a job working for the Ocean City Sanitation Department. We were assistants to the garbage collectors; they had a special process for collecting the garbage. On my first day, Larry told me that we'd have to set all the trash cans out at the end of every driveway. The guys riding on the garbage truck would come behind us and empty the cans. To stay ahead of the truck, we hustled our way from street to street. I wore leg weights all summer to increase my leg strength for basketball. The weights helped my legs and, at the same time, the running helped speed up our work. Almost every night after a full day of trash can prep, we would play basketball.

I returned to school in shape and ready for the season to start. Coach had one goal for our team: to win the state championship. My experience with the little orange ball led me through high school basketball and off to college. I owe everything to that little orange ball.

CHAPTER 2

HOW I GOT THE NAME "HONDO"

There have been lots of *Hondos*—like John Wayne, the movie star, and Frank Howard, a famous Washington Senators baseball player—but none like Ocean City, Maryland's Hondo. That's me! I am often asked how I got the name Hondo. Well, it started in high school. I would watch the NBA's Boston Celtics play basketball. A player named John Hondo Havlicek would hustle all over the court. I admired him for that. He became my favorite player. Hondo wouldn't stop running on defense. I loved his style—he was a very disruptive player on the court. Players on offense couldn't take their eyes off him because he would steal the ball. I decided that I was going to model my style of play after Hondo's. It worked to perfection for me.

I came to school almost every day expressing my excitement about John Hondo Havlicek. One day someone in gym class said:

Stop talking about Hondo. If you don't, your new name is going to be Hondo.

Well, I never stopped. The name Hondo has stuck with me throughout high school, college, and my professional career.

A TRIBUTE TO JOHN HONDO HAVLICEK

While writing my book, I got a text from my good friend, Dr. Beck, around 9:22 p.m. on a spring evening in 2019: *You are the only Hondo. John Hondo Havlicek has just died today, April 25.*

I am so proud of him. I could only think of all the great plays he made during his career. He became an eight-time NBA champion; the 1974 NBA Finals MVP; an eleven-time All-NBA player; and a five-time All-NBA defense player. In 1984, he was inducted into the Basketball Hall of Fame. It's ironic that John Hondo Havlicek's death occurred during my book writing. I was sad to hear of my favorite NBA player's passing.

EXPLAINING MY NAME TO THE KIDS

Most kids today may not know anything about Havlicek. I would always suggest to them that they Google his name. I would say:

If you talked about your favorite basketball player every day, you would understand.

Players like Steph Curry, Lebron James, and Kevin Durant would be great examples of today's favorite basketball stars. Almost every day someone would ask the same question:

How did you get the name Hondo?

My answer has changed over the years, depending on my audience. Addressing the kids, I would share that this NBA basketball player named Hondo was my favorite player. I liked his style of play. To the next generation, I would say:

You know Magic Johnson, right? Suppose you liked Magic Johnson so much that you talked about him all the time. Your friends might start calling you Magic.

I have changed the names over the years, when explaining how I got my name. I have used Michael Jordan, Kobe Bryant, LeBron James, Kevin Durant, then Stephen Curry. It's easier to explain to the kids when they know the players of today. I am happy that Hondo became the name I was known by because everyone in school would call me Alvin instead of Albin, the name my mother gave me.

CHAPTER 3
HOW LUCKY WAS I? TWO MOTHERS!

I consider myself lucky, as I had two mothers and I loved them both. My biological mother, Lola, and the other was my Aunt Helen, my HaHa. My biological mother overcame a lot in her life. Injured early in life, my mother only grew to be around 4'6" tall. That didn't bother her. She still walked down that long road to school along with everyone else. She taught me that helping others is always the right thing to do. That rubbed off on me. Her *never give up* attitude also affected me. She passed her resilience on to me. She encouraged me to be respectful and kind. When she became a beautician, every Saturday our house would be full of ladies waiting to get their hair done. She was always kind to them.

She never saw me play in any sports games. But somehow, she always knew when I got hurt. She would be waiting at the door when I arrived home.

> *I have the hot water waiting for you.*
> *How did you know I got hurt?*
> *Don't worry about it. Just soak your foot and go to bed.*

She was unable to drive, so she relied on our family to take her to the store—family members like Uncle Ralph, HaHa, Cousin James Mumford, plus her friend, Margaret Ann Mumford. She made sure she got rides to 7-Eleven to play the Delaware lottery numbers. Playing the lottery numbers kept her occupied; she became the lottery expert for the community.

People like my cousin Kenny Fooks called her all the time about the lottery. She spent hours figuring out the winning numbers for the week. I still have some of her worksheets.

Colon cancer took a toll on my mother. She went through a terrible operation. She refused chemo treatments after speaking with the doctor.

What are my chances of living if I don't take the chemo?
About 60-40.
Well, I am at 50-50 right now, so I don't want the chemo.

She came to live with us after the operation. We made many trips to her family doctor together. I tried to be strong for her. She was very weak the last time she went to the hospital.

I could only think about what she used to say to me, *You're going to miss me when I'm gone.* This is so true; I miss her every day. I remember sitting next to her in the rehabilitation center, before I left to get some rest. She reached over and squeezed my hand so hard for the longest time. I knew she sent me a signal with that hand grip. A few hours later I got the call. My mother had passed. It felt like my heart stopped beating. She passed on April 16, 2012, at the age of eighty-four. I can't describe how sad I was. I couldn't control my tears. A big part of my life was over. I get so emotional when I think about that day. Then I remember how she believed in me, and that helps me get through each day.

My second mother, HaHa, got her nickname because I couldn't pronounce her name correctly when I was a little boy. HaHa was all that I was able to say for Helen. Some things never change; I still call her HaHa. My family and friends started calling her HaHa. Over the years, the entire community around us started calling her HaHa.

I loved being with her. When her old Plymouth fired up, I was always ready to go with her. It didn't matter where we were going, although I always hoped to get my favorite treat, blueberries. Her friend, Mr. Dave Smith, would come over every Sunday. I must have been no older than five.

HaHa had a tradition of eating ice cream every Sunday. At first, I thought the ice cream was the reason Mr. Dave came over. One night, I guess I got concerned about him. I wondered why he kept coming to eat our ice cream. So I asked him when he was going to go home to eat his own ice cream. My Aunt said, *Mr. Dave, you must get ready to go home to eat your own ice cream.* They later got married.

I started writing this book by researching information about my family. I met with HaHa several times. She told me things that I never knew and showed me pictures that I never had seen before. One was a picture of my great grandfather.

A busy person she was—HaHa was always cleaning her house. She loved keeping her yard manicured. She would always say, *I got things to do,* or *I got a man coming over to fix this.* I am sad to say that HaHa passed on May 30, 2019, at the age of ninety-seven. She lived long enough to see me retire.

Aunt HaHa's children Ronald and Dianna became my big brother and sister. Earlier I mentioned that I am dedicating this book to my brother. I am shedding tears right now because Ronald passed before I completed my book. Another family member became a victim of cancer. He played a major role in my life. I just wanted to follow in his footsteps and be a good person. During a time of segregation, he played for an all-Black school, Worcester High School. He went on to become a successful barber in Philadelphia, Pennsylvania.

Ronald's passing meant I only had my sister Dianna remaining. She took care of me all of my life except for the years when she attended Goldey-Beacom College in Wilmington, Delaware. During my college days, I lived with her one summer. The few times I got in trouble, she helped me take care of the problem. I didn't want to disappoint her. She always showed me a lot of love and still does today.

She tried to protect me even during one of my basketball games. A fight was about to happen, and I could hear her shouting from the stands,

You better not hit my brother! The game had been halted, and she started to come out of the stands. I got her back to her seat and the game continued. She has always been there for me.

She was an enthusiastic cheerleader in high school. She helped lead the student body in singing the *Oh, Worcester* high school song after each basketball game.

MY FATHER

I describe my father, George Alfred Holland, as a proper man—a very proud man who spoke very eloquently. He was a soft-spoken man who pronounced my name Honda instead of Hondo. I never corrected him. Everyone liked him, maybe because he was so delightful to be around. He was easy to get along with. A Korean War veteran who retired from the Army, he returned to Berlin, Maryland to build a home for himself and his mother, Sarah.

My mother never married my father, but I really enjoyed visiting my father. I got to see my brothers, George, James, and Isaac there. He had running water, something that my mother and I didn't have. My dad would often take me different places, mainly to see other family members. He took me swimming one time. It was a very hot, sunny day. I was very young. I could see family members in the water. They seemed to be having lots of fun, splashing water on each other. I didn't want to have any part of that, but my father put me on his shoulders and he began to stride out into this lake. I didn't want to go. I was so nervous; I looked down at the water—it seemed so deep. I remember thinking, *I can't fall into this water because I would surely die.* When he let me go, I started trekking through the water as fast as possible.

I could hear him shouting, *Albin, Come back! It's not that deep.* Afraid for my life, I paid no attention to him. I reached the shore, almost choking from water getting in my mouth. I looked back at my father, who seemed like he was in the middle of the lake. I quickly jumped in the car, soaking wet, and locked the doors, fearing my father would take me back out. It took my father about forty-five minutes to convince me to unlock the car doors.

Unlock the doors, Albin.
No.
I'm not going to take you back out there.

I just kept saying no. We went back and forth with this conversation. He had left his keys inside the car. He convinced me to unlock the door and we went home.

I am not sure why you were so afraid; the water was only about two feet deep. My father told me later that we were only about twenty feet from the shore. We were at one of the many sand holes in our area and not a lake.

Wanting to give back, my father became a Boy Scout leader for our community. He held meetings each week. He would teach the boys lots of things such as the Scout Oath and how to tie a square knot. My cousins were Scouts in his troop. He became a member of the Duncan Showell American Legion Post 231. I later joined the same post's Sons of the American Legion.

My father never saw me play any sports in high school. He didn't see me play in college either. I felt somewhat let down. I would see other players' fathers in the stands and wonder why my dad didn't come. One evening, I asked him why he didn't come to see me play.

He said, *You see those nice tennis shoes you are wearing?*
I said, *Yes.*
Well, I need to get my rest at night to go to work, so I can buy those shoes when you need them.
Come on, Dad, it can't be that hard that you need all that rest.
Okay, since you don't have a game tonight, you're coming with me to work.
I said, *Okay I will be ready. I don't need any rest.*

I will be back before it's time to go.

He went to work about 11:00 p.m. each night. He loved his job in the poultry business as a chicken catcher. His duties included loading chickens into these long trailers. Truck drivers took the trailers filled with chickens back to the poultry processing plant for processing. I came in the house bouncing my ball about two hours before it was time to go to work.

You better get some rest.
That's okay; I'm good.

His boss picked us up that night. Stuffed in the back of this camper truck, I saw six of my father's co-workers. They were all sleeping. When we arrived at the chicken farm, we began working on the first load, picking up three chickens in each hand to be loaded onto the truck. The first thing I noticed was that it seemed hard to breathe…no masks like we wear today. Chicken dust floated in the air; it smelled very bad. These large fans in the chicken houses were supposed to keep the workers cool; however, it was still hot inside the chicken houses. I was sweating right from the beginning. Catching five loads of chicken would take most of the night. At first, I started racing my dad—having fun. The other guys were just looking at me and shaking their heads.

One guy said, *You better slow down, because it will be a long night.*

I just kept trying to beat my dad. About halfway through the first load, I asked my father if I could eat one of the sandwiches that we packed.

Yes, go ahead.

I was starving. I jumped in the back of the truck. Suddenly, I heard a noise. I saw a couple of his co-workers getting in the truck.

I said, *You guys must be hungry, too.*
They said, *No, young fellow, we finished catching all five loads.*

It turns out I slept through the night. My father never said anything about it. I never questioned him again about coming to the games. Lesson learned: *Be careful what you wish for.*

One day at work at the Ocean City Recreation & Parks Department, I got a phone call…a call that touched off the worse day of my life; a call that changed my life forever. Our neighbor called me.

Albin, come home right away! Your dad is being rushed to the hospital in the ambulance.
I am on my way.

I informed my office about the call. My co-worker, Kim Kinsey, consoled me and she offered to drive me to the hospital since I was crying.

No thanks; I can make it.

As I drove onto Coastal Highway, about two blocks away from work, more tears began to roll down my face. Ten blocks later, the tears got worse. I could not stop crying. As I was making my way to Route 90 Bridge, about sixty-five blocks from work, my phone rang. It was a nurse from the hospital.

I am on my way.
Mr. Handy, don't rush. Your father passed five minutes ago.

At that moment, I wished I'd accepted Kim's offer to drive. I was experiencing the worst feeling I'd felt in my entire life. The tears blurred my vision. I could barely see as I crossed the bridge. The realization that I could never talk to my father again hit me. I didn't think I could cry any harder. I don't know how I made it to the hospital. Upon reaching the hospital, I found my dad was already in the morgue. I touched his cold body. I thought about our last discussion.

Stop by when you get off, he had said.

No more pain for my dad. No more problems. No more worries. I said my goodbyes and told him I loved him. Still crying, I let him know that he did a good job raising me and my brothers. I reached out to my wife at work.

Al, I'm so sorry, but it is something we all must go through.

I contacted my brothers to let them know. It was the saddest day of my life. I'm crying as I write about this now. I am feeling the same way I did when my dad passed. Rest In Peace, Dad.

CHAPTER 4

GROWING UP IN BISHOP WITH ONE STORE

My story starts like this: Along with Grandmother Raddie, my Aunt HaHa took my mother to a hospital in Salisbury, Maryland. I think my mother always told me that I was a lucky boy because we were lucky to make it to the hospital. HaHa's vehicle broke down. It seemed the coil wire came loose—again. My aunt jumped out of the car to attach the coil wire. The cars kept honking their horns for her to move. She shouted out:

Stop honking your horns! We need to get to the hospital!

I was born on the 9th day of the snowy month of March. My mother wasn't sure what to name me. A Peninsula Regional Hospital nurse suggested a name.

Why don't you name him Albin, after my husband?

My mother agreed and on that day this Pisces became Albin Anthony Handy.

Even at a young age, I considered family get-togethers to be the highlight of my early years. I looked forward to seeing all my family members at the same time. They came from Maryland, Delaware, Pennsylvania, and California. The adults would shoo us outside with

You kids get outside and play,

and that was just what we wanted to do.

I loved growing up in Bishop on our farmland. Our house was down a long dirt road, and it was surrounded by flourishing peach trees, apple trees, walnut trees, and MomMom's beautiful grape vine. Our land was no more than a stone's throw from the railroad tracks. Trains passed by every day. Sometimes we would put pennies on the track so the trains would flatten them. Why we did this, I don't know. Just something to do, I guess. We weren't thinking about how dangerous it was.

As I mentioned before, our living conditions were not very good. Throughout my childhood, this didn't seem to matter. It didn't matter to many of the families living around me, either. Our conditions seemed normal to me. It didn't take away from what family meant to me. When I went to school...? *That's* when I saw the nice restrooms.

BLUEBERRIES ARE MY BIRTHMARK

One day my mother told me: *Your birthmark is on your right elbow; it's a blueberry.* She explained what a birthmark represented. She said my birthmark made me special and unique. Perhaps my birthmark had something to do with my love for blueberries at an early age. I can remember a story she told me:

My Aunt HaHa drove us to the store one day. After returning home, HaHa and Mom started preparing dinner.

One of them asked the other, *Where is Albin?*

They raced out to the car. There I sat in the back seat with blueberry stains all over me. All the blueberries they'd purchased had been devoured by a hungry little three-year-old. They could only say, *Well, it's our fault! We left him in the back seat.*

I don't think any child labor laws existed back in the day. Mr. Joshua Handy, another cousin, drove us to the blueberry farm each day, starting when I was about eight years old.

I can hear him now: *You children sit down!*

We made sure we obeyed him because he would tell our parents if we didn't. We didn't want to get put off the blueberry bus. I think all my friends worked at the blueberry field. Each summer, I couldn't wait to visit the blueberry field. It was a chance to earn some money. We picked in the scorching hot sun for eight hours every day. When it rained, we would wait under a shelter. Once the pouring rain stopped, we went back to work— sometimes soaking wet, but we made our way back to the fields. It seemed everyone I knew was there.

There always seemed to be a picking competition among my family members. After we picked a full bucket, a field supervisor would give us a ticket showing the bucket's weight. At the end of each day, a supervisor signaled the time by shouting: *Bring your berries up!* We presented each day's tickets at the end of the week to get paid. We wore sweaty, dirty clothes home every day of the week. Purple-colored shoes caked with mud covered our feet all week long in the fields.

We usually rode the bus home. However, sometimes one of my cousins would say, *Let's walk home!* I knew what that meant. They wanted to go by the local pool hall. Shooting pool became a fun thing for us. I'm not sure the owner appreciated us coming in to play when we were so dirty.

Not many people brought their lunch to the blueberry field because this small man named Bill Hutt provided food. He would sell sandwiches, chips, and sodas for lunch. If my memory is correct, he would charge ten cents for each item.

The blueberry field offered little running water and only outhouses. It was a very hot and dirty job, but it was one of the best times for me as a young child.

I was picking with Larry one day when this older girl who knew Larry walked over. I wasn't paying much attention to her. Suddenly, she snatched my ticket from me. I dropped my bucket of blueberries and chased her through the rolls of blueberry bushes. Around and around we went, up and down over the mounds where the blueberry bushes were planted. I just knew I could catch her. After all, I ran everywhere—but I *couldn't* catch up. She stopped next to Larry, only steps away, and just looked at me.

Larry shared later: *I thought Albin was going to fight her because he said there was only one thing left to do. But the next thing he did? He started crying.*

I think I was going to start my first fight to get my ticket back, but I had never been in a fight before and I wasn't going to hit a girl. Undecided on what to do, my emotions just took over. Larry still reminds me of that episode, laughing while he tells the story.

My cousins used to sneak some blueberries to take home, but I wouldn't. They would tease me during our walk home because I would stop at the local grocery store, George's Market, to buy blueberries to take home.

My cousins would ask: *Why are you buying blueberries; you could have taken some from the field?*

I said I would rather buy them, not take them from the owner.

I love blueberries so much that, sixty years later, I have a few bushes planted in my yard.

LIVING ON THE MARYLAND/DELAWARE LINE

In Bishop, we could stroll to our only store in a few minutes. Of course, I would always run there. The Clarence Hammond Store provided everything from gas to hunting licenses to food. Clarence Hammond just happened to be the owner's name, also. Can you believe it? The store was named after the owner. I'm not sure how it happened, but the road next to the store turned out to be Hammond Road!

The two hungry looking German Shepherds lying beside Clarence Hammond's front counter scared me to death. As I rushed past them, he would always say, *They won't bother you.* I never believed him; they had furious barks. When my mother asked me to go to the store, I had to get my courage up. She always wanted me to get a can of Spam, our favorite. I would wait until an adult entered the store, then I would sneak in right next to them. After I made my purchase, I would do the same to get out… wait until someone would leave the store. Don't get me wrong! I liked Mr. Clarence—but I didn't trust his dogs. They always looked like they were waiting for their next meal. I just didn't want to be it. My heart would beat so fast before I left the store, and once I did, I would sprint home as fast as I could.

Besides Mr. Clarence Hammond, another man traveled Hammond Road frequently…this scary truck driver. He made me so nervous whenever I walked—uh, ran—to my Aunt Linda's house. It was only a short distance from our house, but the thought of the scary man driving by made it seem very long. He was a big, mean looking guy who scared all my cousins. He drove this smelly dump truck for the nearby Stink Plant. He seemed to be looking for us every time he drove down Hammond Road, sometimes driving so slowly as if to search us out.

We trembled in our shoes before we jumped the ditch to head down Hammond Road to Aunt Linda's. Every step we took terrified us. Someone would say, *Here comes the scary truck driver!* It felt like Big Foot would soon be chasing us. We could hear his truck roaring behind us. He would bring his big rig to a tire-burning halt and jump out shouting in his deep bass voice: *Come here. I said come here!* He chased us down the road, then got back in his truck. Screaming for our lives, we would jump the big ditch to hide from him. My heart would beat so fast, fearing he might come back. Before we left Aunt Linda's to return home, we started feeling nervous all over again. We were living a nightmare. It seemed like he looked for us every day during the summer. If this scary situation did anything for me, it made me run faster.

Sports became the most important thing for me and my friends after school. We lived only about a mile from each other. A mile seemed like a hop, skip, and a jump when we were young. We decided on the school bus whose house we would visit to play that day. Running to each other's house was something we did every day. Our two communities in Bishop were given names. One was called the Stink Plant; the other—Pig Pen. My friends for life lived in these communities.

The *Stink Plant Boys*—John Ed Mumford, Robert Mumford, Tom Mumford, Wayne Mumford, Willie Paul Mumford, Richard Mumford, Brad Stevens, Barry Johnson, Bobby Spencer, George Knox, Willey Knox, David Mumford—all lived near me. We lived near this awful plant that gave off this bad odor. It's where the scary man worked. Because of the smell, it became known as the Stink Plant. I believe with all my heart that plant polluted our drinking water. Everyone's water was rusty orange looking. Families boiled water for use even before washing their clothes. I can't prove it, but I always believed area residents got cancer from that water.

The *Pig Pen Crew*—Lonnie Mercer, Donnie Mercer, Larry Blake, Russell Blake, Sherret Blake, Gary Cropper, Jerry Tingle, Marlin Waters, Butch Townsend, and Mike Townsend—lived close to the Maryland/Delaware line.

Butch Townsend was known as the best baseball player in our area. He could hit a baseball with tremendous power. You could tell from the crack of the bat when he smashed the ball. Some of his shots could clear Camden Yards. The problem? He crushed the ball so far that sometimes we couldn't find it! With only one ball, the game would be forced to end. I reminded Butch about that recently…how he would stop our baseball game with one swing.

The very popular Pig Pen area included a tavern that everyone would come to on the weekends. We once lived right in front of the tavern. On the weekends there would be many cars parked across the road from our house. Cars sometimes raced down the street at dangerously high speeds, squealing wheels throughout the community. I am sure there was a lot of drinking and driving.

Mom and I moved around the two communities. First, I lived in the Stink Plant area, at my family farm, then we moved to the Pig Pen area, and then back to the Stink Plant area again. The guys would ride me hard because I was the only one who lived in both areas.

Because I grew up just over a mile from the Delaware State Line, we always shopped in Selbyville, Delaware. Although we lived in Maryland, our town was so small that our mailing address was Selbyville. We were allowed to shop in most of their town's stores—but when it came to the restaurants, around the back we went to purchase anything.

Many of my family members lived in Delaware. I played basketball and football there. I even became a Boy Scout in Delaware. I have lots of memories from scouting: competitive day outings, overnight scout camps—and, of course, learning to tie that square knot.

CHAPTER 5

MY GRANDMOTHERS AND GRANDFATHERS

MOMMOM RADDIE

I never met my great-grandmother, Mom Martha. However, my relationship with her daughter—my maternal grandmother—is the gift that keeps on giving. The backbone of our family, she kept us together. We called her MomMom Raddie. (She spelled her name with two *d*s.) When I picture her, I always see her beautiful long hair. I hate to brag, but I would describe her as the greatest grandmother of all time… an amazing lady who instilled her wisdom in me. I loved her so much. It was such an honor to call her my MomMom. She was so well respected in the community. She was the best cook I knew growing up. Sometimes I would call her to ask if she was cooking. She would say, *Come on over. I have plenty of food!* I loved her chicken and dumplings and *no one* could cook a ham like my MomMom. She often cooked an abundance of food because she expected that her grandchildren, like me, would surely be visiting. We all loved our MomMom. Sometimes I would even drive from college to get her dumplings and ham on Sundays.

Her eight children included Aunt Helen (HaHa), Aunt Mildred (Middy), Aunt Ionia, Uncle Wallace (Bud), Uncle Ralph, Uncle Monroe, Aunt Radie (Sis Radie), plus my mother. My Aunt Radie was named after my grandmother, but she spelled her name with one *d*. It seemed like a large family, but it wasn't really. When I was growing up, a large family was ten to fifteen kids.

There are so many great stories I remember about my grandmother. As a kid, I wished I could be as fast and quick as she was. What do I mean by this? Well, a few events come to mind. The first event took place when my grandmother took us to the blueberry field. Everyone picked blueberries during the summer. When lunch time rolled around, our cousin Larry seemed to be finished picking. He started making everyone laugh by playing around. My grandmother walked over to Larry.

She said, *Larry, if you don't stop playing, I'm going to slap you in a minute*. All my cousins started laughing so hard because a funny thing had just happened. In between the words MomMom was saying (*I'm going to* and *slap you in a minute*), she had already slapped him. It went something like this: *Larry if you don't stop playing*—a quick slap across the face, then she finished the statement—*I'm going to slap you a minute*. We couldn't stop laughing. She didn't laugh because she was all about the business of picking blueberries.

The second event occurred when all my cousins came to my MomMom's second house. One of my cousins, Charles—whose nickname was Puggy—decided to walk home. All my cousins kept telling him he couldn't go home yet.

My MomMom shouted, *Puggy, come back! Your mother is not home.*
He responded with, *No, I'm going home anyway*
He started jogging towards home. As he looked back, he mumbled, *She can't catch me.*

He put some distance between himself and her house. I think he thought he would make it home. However, by the time he turned around a second time, my grandmother was grabbing him by the shoulder. We all stood in amazement at how our MomMom ran him down. We never doubted our grandmother again. She raced him down so fast that it shocked him. When she brought him back, she asked, *Does anyone else wanted to run away?* You could hear a pin drop. I decided I would never try to run away from my MomMom, because she was just too fast. I think I may have inherited some of my speed from her.

I guess I got my work ethic from her too. She used to work from sunup to sundown on our farm. Regardless of the weather conditions, she put in a full day.

There are so many events my MomMom played a special part in throughout my young life. Larry and I often stayed with my MomMom on Sunday nights. MomMom would begin cooking dinner early. She would be expecting some of our family members. When they arrived she would say, *You boys go in the back room.* We knew what that meant: *Be quiet.*

Larry was so funny. He would say, *I hope they don't eat all the food up.* At the end of dinner, they would start a conversation. It never failed; Larry would get me laughing so loudly that we would get in trouble every time the family gathered.

Here's how the story went: Larry would say,
Listen! MomMom is going to say the same things she says every Sunday.
A family member would say something, then Larry would say,
Wait—just listen! MomMom is going to say, 'Shut up or don't tell it.'

It was just the way our older people talked back then.

An example would be that someone would say something like,
Did you know this certain person left his wife?
MomMom would respond with, *Shut up.*
Larry would say, *Does MomMom want the people to talk, or does she want them to shut up? I don't understand.*

I would immediately start laughing.

And if our family member said the same thing:
Did you know that so-and-so left his wife?

MomMom would say, *Don't tell it.*

Larry would say, *Does MomMom want them to tell her or not?*

By now I would be in a full-out crying laugh. He just wouldn't stop talking about MomMom. I couldn't stop laughing until I'd hear her say, *Excuse me—I will be right back.* She would come in the back room. Larry would get in trouble because she knew he was the one who started it. He always said that I got him in trouble, but it was Larry who started it.

We learned a lot from our MomMom. She taught family members how to cook and how to raise a family. She never let us down; when she spoke, we all listened. MomMom—thanks for everything. The photo of us at my college graduation is still my favorite.

GRANDFATHER WALLACE

I never met my grandfather on my mother's side of the family. He was described to me as a hardworking man. My aunt said, *He was a man with very strict rules that he never went back on.* He owned a lot of land in the area. He even had a farm located at the family place; everyone called it *Up House.* Family members worked on the farm. Our food came from our fields. It didn't matter what the weather was like; our grandfather was always working. Because I never met him, I relied on what my family members told me about him. I do remember his brother, Uncle Lenford. My cousins cut grass for him at private homes and local businesses, so I wanted to cut also. One day Uncle Lenford decided to give me a try. I worked hard to get the lawn at a local business cut while my uncle was running some errands. When he came back, he fired me. I had just finished cutting my first lawn and he said, *You don't know how cut grass.* Devastated, I walked about two miles back home. Still dumbfounded and wondering how I lost my first grass cutting job, I just couldn't figure it out. To me grass cutting was grass cutting. I suppose I didn't have the skills. When I ride by that building today, the memories of that day still come back to me.

GRANDMOTHER SARAH

My Grandmother Sarah—or Mom Sarah, as many called her—took care of the house my dad built. She kept the house organized until her grandsons decided to wrestle through the rooms. Our grandmother cooked some great breakfasts. In the mornings, she always asked, *Do you boys want pancakes or French toast?* My favorite was French toast. I don't think my brothers cared. We would start shouting out our choices as we raced to get in the bathroom first. To my grandmother, the majority always won. Most of the time, my brothers agreed on breakfast choices anyway. We knew when it was almost time to eat because the entire house smelled so good. We couldn't wait to get to the table. I can hear my grandmother calling, *Come to breakfast.* After breakfast, she would start to get ready for work. Before she walked out the door she would say, *You boys keep the house clean while I am at work.* I remember seeing her sitting, reading the Bible before going to work each morning.

My grandmother cleaned hotels in Ocean City, Maryland. This big van would pick her up along with other mothers and grandmothers in the community. They each would climb the hotel stairwells to prepare at least five to six rooms each day. Cleaning the rooms included changing sheets and pillowcases, vacuuming, cleaning the bathroom, and taking out the trash. She would leave for work around 9:00 in the morning. I would watch my brothers when my grandmother went to work. My father would get home by 11:00 a.m. My grandmother would then return home around 2:00 p.m. and start preparing dinner. It appeared that she worked all the time. If not cooking or cleaning the house, she would be heading to Ocean City to clean hotel rooms.

I loved visiting my grandmother; it gave me another opportunity to spend time with my brothers. I was their big brother, and they listened to me—for the most part.

Grandmother Sarah had this pear tree in the backyard that served as the pole for our basketball rim. That pear tree produced large pears each year. My brothers and I would play for hours, then eat pears for a while. I'm not sure it was real basketball because I challenged all three of my brothers. They would hold my arms and legs, jump on my back—do anything to try to stop me from making a basket.

My grandmother felt it was important that I be educated about our community and all my family members living there. We lived on Branch Street; she wanted me to know everyone who lived around us. When we took walks down the street, it seemed like everyone we saw was related. The Hollands, the Jarmons, the Purnells, the Brittinghams all lived there.

As I met the neighbors, they would say, *Hi cousin!* I looked at my grandmother the first time this happened.

Albin, say 'Hello, cousin!'
I said, '*Hello cousin*,' not really knowing them.

In Berlin, I don't remember hearing people in the community refer to adults as aunts or uncles; instead, they called everyone *Mom* or *Pop*. If someone was addressing my grandmother, they would probably call her *Mom Sarah*. If someone was asking about my dad, they would ask how *Pop Alfred* was doing. This is something that is still carried on today. My Berlin family is a close-knit family. Everyone knows everyone.

When I got older and started having girls coming around, my grandmother would ask them, *Who are your people?* Before I knew it, she would be telling me and the girls that we were cousins, so we couldn't be dating. After a while, I didn't want to bring my girlfriends around.

Weekend visits with my grandmother meant church on Sunday morning. My brothers George and James and I followed her down to church every Sunday. We walked down Branch Street to St. Paul's United Methodist Church. When my other brother Isaac visited from his home in Delaware, he would also have to go to church. After church, we were ready to get home. We would rush to take off our Sunday clothes before we started to play ball.

GRANDFATHER EDWARD

Later in life, I got to know my Grandfather Edward. We called him Granddad. My Grandmother Sarah parted ways with him a long time ago. He moved to Phoenixville, Pennsylvania, but visited maybe every four years. When he did visit, I didn't interact with him much. After the death of my grandmother, he decided to return home to live with my dad. He stayed out back in a little place behind our house.

Granddad was a very funny man who loved watching television. He enjoyed all the old cowboy shows. His favorites were *The Lone Ranger, The Virginian,* and *The Rifleman.* He gazed at the television with great intensity, as if he was an actor waiting to give his input. This happened a lot when he watched the show *Sanford and Son.* You would hear him talking to characters on the show, warning them: *Don't go in that room.* The person on television would go in the room. You would hear gun shots. My Granddad would say, *I told you not to go in there, you big dummy; I told you. You didn't listen.* We would laugh every time. He held conversations with the actors throughout the shows. He would be so mad at their characters. He warned them, but they wouldn't listen.

When he decided to stay in Berlin, I could see how happy it made my father. They were like two young schoolmates. With my father still working at night, it became a problem. The two of them often enjoying spirits late into the evening... That meant my father would have to cut their time short to rest for work. One day my father said to me, *I think I am going to retire to spend more time with my dad.* I asked him if he was sure he wanted to do that. He said, *I think so.*

His happiness was short-lived. Just a few months after my father retired, my Granddad passed. I remember it like it was yesterday. After watching television, he decided to go lie down for a while. Within a few minutes, my brother Ike went to check on him. He was not breathing. We called for an ambulance. EMTs pronounced him dead. This took a toll on my father— one that he never overcame.

CHAPTER 6
OUR FAMILY HOUSE—"UP HOUSE"

Most of my aunts and uncles grew up in this special house in Bishop. This two-story family house became the place for our family to meet. A long, dusty dirt road took us back to the place we called Up House. It was surrounded by our farmland. MomMom Raddie's children spent their childhood there and raised many of their kids there. Before you got back to Up House, there was a much smaller house where MomMom cooked. We called it *The Shop*. It housed MomMom's restaurant named *Handy's Lunch Bar*. She decided to open Handy's Lunch Bar because chicken truck drivers were unable to purchase food from the other restaurants. MomMom sold food to them, and soon other people from up and down the East Coast began to stop at Handy's for a meal.

One of my fondest memories about Up House was a Christmas story that I must share. At a young age, I loved Christmas and believed in Santa Claus. On a certain Christmas Eve, I was determined to see Santa. In Up House stood a beautiful Christmas tree, all decorated. The tree was in the back room, next to the couch where I was laying. No one could convince me to go to bed, not even my mother. She said, *Come to bed! Santa will be here later.* I remember saying that I wanted to see Santa. She went upstairs to bed. My uncles and aunts were still in the kitchen. I knew there were no presents under the tree, so I wanted to see Santa delivering the presents. I just laid there with my eyes open, waiting. I don't know how long I was awake, but I must have fallen asleep. Suddenly, I opened my eyes to see presents under the tree. I was so sad. I ran up the steps to wake my mother, while starting to tear up. She said, *What's wrong, Albin?* I could only tell her I had missed him again. She said, *You will have to try again next year.*

When our family assembled in Up House, my cousins would play some type of game we invented. We loved playing together all day. We challenged each other in races around the house. Some of us decided to run in the opposite direction—not a good idea, especially when it was getting dark. I collided with one of my cousins head-on. The swelling on my forehead turned into a knot that looked like a golf ball. Now I wonder if I had a concussion. Sometimes sprinting around the house lasted for a long time—well, until we got tired.

Cowboys and Indians became a favorite game of mine. My cousin once said, *I shot you in the eye, Albin.* I told him I could still see him with my other eye. In the dirt we designed Tic-Tac-Toe games and Hopscotch diagrams. We played Hide-and-Go-Seek and kickball in the fields. In kickball, we made up our own rules. Jump rope competitions kept us active, as we learned all the Double Dutch jumps and the different styles of jumping. A basketball court stood in the backyard. My friend Charles would make small holes in the ground so we could play golf. We used a rubber ball, no golf balls, and a stick as our golf club. Lots of fields with tall grass surrounded the house. When dusk came, we would catch lightening bugs. One thing was sure…we didn't sit around in the house. We didn't have much, but there was always lots to do.

CHAPTER 7

MEMORIES—AUNT LINDA, UNCLE WILL, UNCLE BEN & MORE

GREAT AUNTS

I don't remember much about my great aunts. I do remember Great Aunt Linda. Looking at Great Aunt Linda, I saw a carbon copy of my MomMom. We spent a lot of time going over to Great Aunt Linda's home. Her husband, Elisha, had lots of farmland where they grew their food. I wanted to learn to drive his tractor, but I was too young. When I ran over to her house, I was very careful not to step on any of his plants that were in the field. Her children were Marie (Roxie), Tody, Pelp, Estella, Benny, Linda, and Wanda. Later in my life, my mother and I lived across the road from Great Aunt Linda in a house that my Aunt HaHa once lived in.

GREAT UNCLES

I can't remember everything about my great uncles either. I do know that they were all short in stature, just like me. I do remember lots of good family fun time with them. All couple of our great uncles lived in Philadelphia and near Wilmington, Delaware. They would make the long drives to come see my MomMom on the weekends.

Uncle Will was a smooth Philly Slicker. He dressed in his Sunday clothes every day. He kept a pocket full of money. We raced to find him once we found out he was in town. We knew he was going to give us a few dollars. In fact, he showed us the first $100 bill that we had ever seen.

Our very interesting Uncle Ben enjoyed life to the fullest. He loved the spirits of life. His goal was always to visit my MomMom after he made the long drive. Sometimes, however, he didn't make it. Uncle Ben would drive some 110 miles from Wilmington, then stop at the Pig Pen Tavern— less than a mile from my MomMom—and never make it to see her. After being up all night, he would sometimes drive back to Wilmington. I don't think he wanted my MomMom to see him after partying. He did sometimes visit his grandchildren, Larry, Bernida, Gary, and Monique in nearby Berlin.

We loved all our family members. There were plenty of other great uncles, such as Uncle Elisha, Uncle Isaac, Uncle Ike, Uncle Lee Rogers, and Uncle John. Uncle Will and Uncle Ben were the ones I remembered the most about. My great uncles all seemed to be from around 5' to 5'7". I think I got my height from them.

CHAPTER 8

LESSONS LEARNED FROM MY AUNTS AND UNCLES

MY AUNTS

What can I say about my aunts? I can say that every one of my aunts felt like my other mother from time to time. Have you ever heard the expression *It takes a village*? I was always over at one of my four aunts' houses, I suspect, because they all had children. My family was so big that it really did take a village to raise the kids. When I visited my aunts, I became a member of their families. I respected them like they were my mother and father. I listened to everything they said to me. I really didn't have a choice.

AUNT HELEN (HAHA)

HaHa was the oldest of my grandmother's children. At times, she would take on many of my grandmother's duties to help the family. I stayed over at her house probably more than I stayed at my mother's house. HaHa was always doing something for her brothers and sisters, helping with their children. I loved her so much. I would sit on our step to wait for her to come home at lunchtime. I would be so excited when I saw her car. I would jump off the step to have lunch with her. I went everywhere with her. When her car started up, I expected to go with her, and I was so disappointed when I couldn't go. She said, *Many people thought you were my son*. She would take me to see her son's basketball games. That's when I began to learn the rules of basketball. When the basketball officials blew their whistles, I started to understand why. These were some of the most exciting times of my life.

As a supervisor, my aunt got me a job at H & H Poultry Factory. She even offered to pick me up to take me to work. But she had a stipulation: I needed to be organized and ready to go. She said, *I will pick you up from your mother's house at 7:00 a.m.* I remember this because the sun would just be coming up. She said, *I will blow the horn twice: once when I arrive and the second time when I turn around.*

The first day, I was very nervous sitting at the front door, hoping I didn't fall asleep. *I must be ready if I want a ride. If not, I'll have to run about a mile to the factory.* Each morning, I would be ready: boots on, apron in hand, listening for HaHa's horn.

One day I was waiting by the door, and I must have dozed off. I looked at the clock: 7:15! I jumped up shaking, and I shouted to my mom.

Why didn't you wake me up?
I heard her answer…*What?*

I was gone in a flash, sprinting as fast as I could towards the factory and sweating harder with every stride. I just knew my aunt would fire me if I didn't get there as fast as I could. I reached the gate to go to work. The security guard, Mr. Emp Showell, stopped me: *Where are you going?* I told him I was late and that my Aunt HaHa left me because I fell asleep.

I have to go; I'm already late!
Wait! When did you start working the night shift?
Night shift. What do you mean?
He responded, *Yes, this is the night shift. Did you mean you thought this was the morning shift?*
I said, *Oh no. Please don't tell my aunt!*
I won't; you don't have to worry about it. Just go get some rest.

Guessing he had seen this happen before, I felt pretty good that he wouldn't say anything. Although I wasn't positive that he would keep our secret, I had his word.

Here's what happened: After working all day, I came home. However, I only made it as far as the chair I sat in every morning—the chair that I waited in for my aunt each morning. I still had my boots on, and my apron was next to me. When I woke up, the sun was going down. It looked the same to me as it did in the morning. I just figured I was late for work. Instead of being 7:15 a.m., it was 7:15 p.m.! I usually ran everywhere I went. But that day, I walked all the way back home frustrated about this unbelievable and embarrassing mistake. If Larry and Junie found out about it, they would never let me live it down. As I got closer to home, I began to smile about the funny mistake I had made. My mom stood at the door waiting for me, as she always did. I told her I thought it was in the morning. She said, *I wondered what you were talking about. I didn't know where you went. You were so tired when you came in that I didn't bother you.* I was so embarrassed that I went to bed. At least my aunt didn't know. I made sure I heard my aunt blow the horn the next day.

When I came outside, she asked, *Are you okay?*
I said, *Yes.* I must have looked nervous.
The next thing she said shocked me. *You want to ride with me, or do you want to run to work?*

At that moment I knew that the security guard had contacted my aunt. She started to laugh; I started to smile. How many other family members would hear this story? Every time I saw that security guard at the store or anywhere else, he would ask if I was still trying to work the night shift.

I always trailed along behind one of my cousins—this time it was Larry and we ended up in the community called Pig Pen. I must have been about eight years old at the time. My cousin knew this lady who lived next to one of our friends, Larry Blake. She owned a big chest full of old jewelry. I am not sure if the jewelry was valuable because the box sat outside unlocked. Anyway, he encouraged me to go in her backyard with him to see the jewelry. It didn't look very good, so we left. We took one of our traditional routes back home…the railroad track. I don't think the trains were scheduled that day, so we were safe. Besides, we could hear if a train was coming. Walking on the rails again, we were trying to balance ourselves all the way home—a challenging game we loved trying. We reached our farmland and climbed the hillside. We started our familiar walk towards Up House. As we approached our grandmother's house, we could see our Aunt HaHa standing at the back door. She said, *You boys come on in. Go in the back room.* We wondered what was wrong. I noticed that all our adult family members seemed to be in the front room. It seemed like about thirty minutes before she came to the back room.

She said, *I don't know what you boys did. I just don't know if we will be able to help you.* She left the room again.

I asked my cousin, *Do you think she is talking about us going in the lady's jewelry box?* I can't remember how he responded. In about another thirty minutes, she came back.

She said, *It looks like you two are going to go to the Children's Home.* Today it might be described as a group home or youth treatment center.
I said to myself, *The Children's Home?*

Back in the day, kids sent to the Children's Home never returned. Bad kids went there for years. I was so scared; I kept thinking about our potential fate. I couldn't believe it—the thought that we might be sent away. It seemed like another about thirty minutes before my aunt came back.

She said, *We have been talking to the people from the Children's Home. If you tell them what happened, they will see what they can do.*

I couldn't wait to tell them everything. She left the room again.

When she came back this time, she said, *They are going to give you a break this time, but the next time it will be too late.*

I think she told us to go to sleep. I thought about what we had done. That lesson stayed with me all my life. If it's not yours, don't even think about taking someone's property. Lesson learned.

AUNT MILDRED (MIDDY)

My Aunt Middy enjoys life; she always did. She celebrates her 98th birthday this year. No one would believe it, but she still dances like a young adult. I love Aunt Middy. She is known for saying, *Give me my flowers while I am living.* She is so funny. As the old folks used to say, she didn't let any grass grow under her feet. She lived in many places, including Maryland, Delaware, and Philadelphia, Pennsylvania.

When she lived in Bishop, I loved being at her house. I enjoyed being with all her children. Sometimes I didn't want to go home…I guess because of all the fun things we did. I learned a lot from her two oldest sons, Larry and Junie. Larry was an all-around athlete who fell in love with the Beatles. Junie was a standout distance runner in high school. He became one of the best in the state. Larry could run also. He once ran two miles to the store after school to buy a Beatle wig. Members of the popular English rock band, the Beatles, all wore long hair. This made them stand out from any other groups. The thought of wearing a Beatles wig to school intrigued Larry. The next day Larry wore the wig, and the bus driver wouldn't let him on the bus.

My best friend, Charlie Milbourne, lived next door to me. We always played some type of ball with Larry and Junie: football, baseball, or basketball. I don't know if we played with a football or not. I know we used a stick as our baseball bat. We used a worn-out rubber ball. Most of the time our rubber basketballs didn't last long. We played with basketballs that sometimes-lost air during the games.

I would spend a lot of time over at my Aunt Middy's house...so many cousins to play with! Lillian, who we called Lil, became like a sister to me. She became one of my mom's favorites. Aunt Middy's children—Larry, Junie, Lillian, Demetrice, Franchito, Concepcion, Augustine, Aparicio, Brenda, and Leon—were very close.

AUNT IONIA

I thought my Aunt Ionia's long hair made her look so beautiful. I loved visiting her and my cousins in Frankford, Delaware. I felt right at home when I stayed there. Aunt Ionia treated me just like I belonged to her. With two sets of bunk beds and her three boys, I fit right in. The fourth bunk became mine when I slept over.

Peanut vines grew in her backyard. I couldn't believe it—a peanut vine on the Eastern Shore. I wondered if my cousins' favorite snack might have been peanut butter sandwiches. A huge grapevine grew beautiful purple grapes each summer. There was this wide creek that bordered their land, way in their backyard. We sometimes used these running vines to swing across the embankments. We were lucky the vines didn't break because we would have been in trouble with all that water.

I wanted to share my basketball knowledge with Aunt Ionia's oldest son, Frank. That became my focus for one summer when I stayed with them. He worked hard trying to learn the fundamentals of the game. He learned how, why, and when to pass, dribble, shoot, and rebound. We practiced his newly learned skills in basketball games against his neighborhood friends.

Along with learning to write, spell, add, and speak, my mother taught me how to cook. So I taught Frank how to cook Spam. He couldn't believe it. He was so surprised and kept saying, *Albin knows how to cook!* I don't think my aunt allowed him anywhere near the kitchen. I take that back; he could make a mean peanut butter and jelly sandwich! He had plenty of practice because I think we ate that sandwich every day during the summer.

I remember going to Frank's Little League games. There was no organized baseball where I lived, so Frank asked the coach if I could play. I didn't know anything about the age limit. I was much smaller than Frank, but I was two years older. I don't think the coach thought about asking my age, and he allowed me to play. I only played for a few innings. Playing third base, I made a couple good plays on hard-hit balls. I collected a couple of good hits. The coach asked me my age. After I told him, he said I was too old to continue to play. I was so disappointed that I walked back to my aunt's house by myself. That "almost" opportunity sparked my interest in the game. I decided that I was going to play on a baseball team one day.

A few years later, Aunt Ionia decided to move to Maryland. I couldn't have been happier. I was so excited because Frank would be enrolling in my school. I made sure my basketball coach knew my cousin Frank wanted to play basketball. This meant that we would be playing basketball on the same court. I competed as a member of the varsity team. He would compete on the junior varsity team. I became his biggest cheerleader at the games.

My Aunt Ionia married Frank Marshall, Sr. Their six children were Geraldine, Teresa, Cynthia, Frank, Bruce, and Brian. In high school, all the boys played sports. Frank and Brian both played basketball, while Bruce ran track. Cynthia became a favorite of my mom's and like another sister to me. She called me her cousin/brother.

AUNT SIS RADIE

For a long while, we lived next door to my Aunt Sis Radie. (She spelled her name differently than her mother—she used one *d*.) To visit her, I would dash out our back door. I would be at her front door in less than seven seconds. I tried to beat that record many times. I spent many days and nights at my Aunt Sis Radie's house. I was always happy to be there for breakfast since she cooked the best eggs that I ever tasted. I'm not sure what ingredients she added, but to me her eggs were award-winning.

Aunt Sis Radie influenced me because she spent a lot of time writing. She wrote about historical events and influential people such as Martin Luther King. She also wrote poetry. Her son, Kevin, later published some of her writings. The book, *Roses Signifies the Grace of God,* is available on Amazon.

Aunt Sis Radie's husband, Charles Fooks, had a love of cars. Many times when I visited, he would fire up one of his many vehicles and off to Ocean City we would go. It was so exciting to cross the Harry Kelly Bridge. What I didn't like was when we had to stop on the bridge. You could see the water through the road grates. I wasn't happy with that; it was scary. Sitting on that bridge looking down in the water put fear in our hearts. The other thing that frightened us came when the bridge opened to allow the big boats to go to the other side. All the boats in the water were beautiful, but that didn't stop us from being nervous when we looked down. Once we crossed the bridge and headed into Ocean City, we felt safe.

Uncle Charles would drive down Wicomico Street, where his side of the family lived. I remember it just like it was yesterday. This is where my Uncle Charles' mother, sister, and brother lived. I think I did my first ever crabbing with their oldest son, Charles (Puggy). On the way home, we would stop by the local drive-in movie. Located on Route 50 going out of Ocean City, this was the only drive-in movie in the area. We just stopped along the highway to see the movie. I guess either we weren't allowed to go, or we didn't have enough money. We watched the movie for a while without being able to hear anything. Oh, well…it was still exciting to us.

Uncle Charles' and Aunt Sis Radie's children Charles (Puggy), Kenny, Kevin, and Etta (Darlene) were all good athletes and they all partic-ipated in sports. In high school, Puggy wrestled and Kenny played baseball and football, while Kevin played football and was a great basketball player. Kenny went on to win Most Valuable Player in baseball for the University of Maryland Eastern Shore. Darlene was an outstanding gymnast in high school. She used her athleticism to become cheerleader at the college level for the University of Maryland Eastern Shore. I'm so proud of her; she now works at Buckingham Elementary School.

MY UNCLES

My mother's three brothers were all special in their own way. I felt it would be appropriate to mention something unique about each of them. We called them Uncle Wallace (Bud), Uncle Ralph, and Uncle Monroe.

UNCLE WALLACE (BUD)

Uncle Wallace was named after my grandfather. However, we all called him Uncle Bud. When he started building his house, I could barely see over the bricks of his foundation. I couldn't have been any older than five or six. For some reason he asked me,

> *Do you think I should marry Mildred?* (She was his companion.)
> I remember asking him, *What's marriage?*
> He explained so I could kind of understand.
> I remember saying, *Yes, I think you should marry her.*

Uncle Bud was known throughout our family for being the neatest man we'd ever met. He was always cleaning everything he touched…always wiping his hands. My uncle owned Handy's T.V. Repair Shop. People from all around would bring their televisions to him…the ones with those big tubes inside. From time to time, I worked for him changing the smaller tubes and soldering the loose wires. He had his employees keep a timesheet on these small pieces of paper. I recorded 15 minutes here and 30 minutes there. I don't remember how much we got paid per hour. If we ate lunch at his house, a certain amount would be subtracted from our pay. I don't think we got paid until Fridays. His number one worker, Brad Stevens, became a family friend.

As I mentioned before, my Uncle Bud liked things clean and neat. He used these special paper towels to wipe things in his shop. He wouldn't let us throw them away; instead, he asked us to wash them and hang them to dry. He never wanted to waste anything.

He also drove a school bus for years. He spent a short period in the military. He used his military skills to keep his students in line on his bus. Cleaning his bus kept us busy on the weekends.

His wife, Aunt Mildred, became a schoolteacher. They had two boys and one girl: Wallace, Wilson (Bill), and Wynette. Wynette and Wilson were twins; Wilson died at an early age. Wallace became another wrestler in the family. Wynette is now an assistant principal at Worcester Technical High School.

UNCLE RALPH

I will always be so thankful for my Uncle Ralph. He helped my mother with whatever she needed. Although short in stature, like the rest of our family, Uncle Ralph was a very muscular human being and the strongest man I knew. So many muscles seemed to be all over his body. No one seemed to mess with him. When they did, they only did it one time. He worked various jobs. One summer, I worked with him installing some bulkheading in Ocean Pines, just outside of Ocean City. I lifted those heavy sheets, one at a time, then I carried them down to the water's edge to my uncle. I liked physical work because to me it was like training for basketball. But that physical heavy lifting job seemed almost too much. It was some of the hardest work I have ever done in my life—but I never quit. I made it through the entire summer.

I remember this guy kept bothering my uncle on the job. Uncle Ralph said, *You need to stop bothering me; my nephew is here.* That guy kept bothering him. My uncle said, *Let's just work.* Well, the guy kept bothering him. The next thing I knew my uncle lifted him over his head. He tossed him in the water. I just stood there—watching and wondering what had happened.

The guy got up and said, *Man I was just playing.*
My uncle said, *This is not a time to be playing because I am at work.*

He said that the guy never messed with him again.

Uncle Ralph helped build the Route 90 bridge that leads into Ocean City. I remember seeing the bridge when it wasn't done, watching the builders work. They seemed to be hanging in mid-air. My uncle told us that he never got nervous working on the bridge. Just looking at that bridge so high made my legs tremble. I was so scared that I knew I never wanted to do that type of work.

I loved Uncle Ralph's fancy moves on the basketball court; he was so inspiring to me. He loved his companion, Jackie. Their children were Ralph (Little Ralph), Dwayne, Marlynn, Bernard, Vonna, and Ernestine. Dwayne played basketball in high school. Vonna played volleyball in high school. She finished her volleyball career playing four years for Morgan State University.

UNCLE MONROE

Uncle Monroe took the long shots on the basketball court. I always admired him for that, but I couldn't figure out how he did it. Of course, I was so young that I couldn't understand much anyway. He served his time after being drafted into the Army. Upon returning home, he completed barber school training in Philadelphia. He then opened his barber shop in the City of Brotherly Love, where he still lives and runs that barber shop today. His first marriage with Delores brought them one child, Sharon.

I enjoyed visiting him during the summer. I met his wife's little brother. He and a group of neighborhood boys jumped some guy and started beating him up. He asked me to join in, but I wouldn't. We didn't get along after that.

I remembered when my Uncle Monroe and Delores came home to visit us in Bishop. After the week ended, they were about to leave. I have always remembered when Delores said,

Monroe, can I stay another week down in the country?
My uncle said, *Put your luggage in the car and we will talk about it.*

I think she enjoyed her time with Aunt Middy

His second wife's name was named Sharon. Their son was Monroe (Junior) and they adopted a daughter, Verne'e. Sharon also had a son named Ralph.

My friend Robert Mumford and I attended the Jack Kraft Basketball Camp in Greenland, Pennsylvania. Jack Craft was the head basketball coach at Villanova University at the time. I gave it my all during that week. I worked so hard as the point guard for my team. My team won the camp championship and I received my first trophy ever. After the game, I received my first basketball collegiate offer to Elmira College, Elmira, New York. I was so excited that my team won the championship and that I had an offer to play basketball in college. I couldn't wait to get home to show everyone my trophy. I also couldn't wait to show my uncle the trophy. He picked us up at the bus station in Philadelphia. When I showed him my trophy and told him about my experience at camp, he said, *Congratulations, you must have done a great job.* That felt good coming from him, a former player. We spent a couple days with him before taking the bus home.

I am so proud of Uncle Monroe. Of all the people living in Philadelphia, he was asked to open the third session of the Democratic National Convention on July 27, 2016. He recited the Pledge of Allegiance on the evening Hillary Clinton claimed the Democratic Party nomination for president.

CHAPTER 9

EXCITING TIMES WITH MY COUSINS

I'm not sure why we enjoyed being around each other so much, but we sure did look forward to it. We took full advantage of our time together. When my cousins assembled at MomMom's, it sometimes seemed like twenty of us. We never sat around the house. We were expected to go outside. We were told to get outside. Our parents didn't want us inside. Grown folks would be talking inside.

No one in our family ever purchased any sporting equipment. We either made our own or found something to play with. Monopoly and the game of Jacks came later. With no direction, we were able to stay busy all day. Water from our outside hand pump kept us hydrated. We played all the time. Our main running game was tag, with kickball a strong second. Can you imagine all my cousins—at least a dozen—running to avoid being tagged?

When it was time to go, some of my cousins would try to hide, hoping they would be able to stay. One of my aunts got all the way home to Frankfort, Delaware before realizing someone was missing. None of her children said anything until she asked, *Where is Cynthia?* She then realized she had left her daughter at MomMom's. Then, in a panic, she raced down U.S. 113 to pick her child up.

My cousin Lillian would also slip away. She would sneak over to our house. My mother would be glad to see her. Sometimes no one knew she was gone for a long while. Then her mother, Aunt Middy, would figure it out and come looking for her. Lillian knew she was in trouble so she would try to hide.

I think that my cousins had so much fun that we didn't want the fun to stop. I couldn't stop thinking about the next time we would get together.

CHAPTER 10
MY LOVE FOR BASKETBALL BEGINS

Getting hooked on the game of basketball became a blessing in my life. It was truly life changing. Whenever I heard the swishing sound as the ball went through the net, for some reason I felt excited. If a player made a couple shots in a row, he was considered hot. Teammates would say *He is on fire!* and shout *Get him the ball! The basket seems to be so big to him.* These are all comments I would hear the players saying about their teammates. Watching my uncles Ralph and Monroe play taught me valuable lessons. Even at a young age, I could watch them play basketball all day. I studied them week after week. You see, I was too young to make a basket. There were no portable basketball goals that could adjust the basket short enough for me. But the desire to make a goal was there. When I bounced a basketball on their dirt court, there was a mighty bounce I wouldn't forget. One day—a basket would happen for me. Until then, I would watch my uncles play with great concentration. My Uncle Ralph's fantasy shots; my Uncle Monroe's long jump shots…I certainly admired how they played with two different styles. They played so much that the dirt surface on their yard court be came almost level.

CHAPTER 11
CHURCH AND THE LONE RANGER

Let's go, Albin. Are you ready? It's time to go!

My Aunt HaHa would call to me each Sunday that I stayed with her. We traveled to Selbyville, Delaware, making the turn towards Zoar Methodist Church. This meant many things. It meant seeing family members from both Maryland and Delaware. It meant Sunday School Class was about to begin. It meant Sunday Service would soon follow.

I loved Sunday School. I participated in all the different plays during the holidays. I remember learning my Easter poems. I practiced over and over, sometimes in front of my family, but I was still nervous going on stage when it came to speaking. Looking out at the audience, I just saw so many people. My challenge each Sunday?—trying to get my Aunt HaHa to leave church. I wanted her to hurry and get us home. I needed to watch The Lone Ranger. I would always do my best to encourage my aunt to leave. However, the post-church discussions always occurred—HaHa was greeting people she saw last week as if she hadn't seen them in a month.

Come on HaHa, let's go! Tonto and the Lone Ranger await.
In a moment, Albin. I am talking.

She didn't understand how important it was to me. I had to see the masked man and his partner!

CHAPTER 12
MY PRESCHOOL STARTED AT HOME

Back in the day, the only preschool came from your parents at home. Mothers did their best to prepare their kids for their first educational experience away from home. First grade teachers at school would provide their first experience with instructors other than their parents.

My mother worked with me drilling each letter of the alphabet so I could recognize and name all of them, showing me over and over how to write each letter. My Aunt Mildred, an elementary school teacher, said that I could write her name when I was just three years old! I loved practicing how to add and subtract with my mother. Perhaps that is why I enjoyed elementary school.

My mother would spend hours working with me, teaching me how to spell, how to write, how to talk, and how to act. I can still hear her talking. Perhaps that's why I loved Flower Street Elementary School so much. I couldn't wait to go to school each morning.

My mother said, *I am confident that you are ready for school.* I remembered that through elementary, high school, and college.

CHAPTER 13

MY LOVE FOR FLOWER STREET ELEMENTARY SCHOOL

ELEMENTARY SCHOOL EXPERIENCE

My school bus couldn't arrive fast enough for me. I sat on our step early in the morning anticipating that yellow bus every single school day. I still remember my first day of elementary school. I was so excited to meet my teacher. My cousin Larry directed me to the little building for first, second, and third-grade classes. Some children cried on their first day of school. I wasn't sure why. I fell in love with my school on the first day. I had never seen that many kids my age at the same time. First and second graders were in my class. That small classroom building still stands today.

The role those teachers played in my life cannot be measured—teachers like my first-grade teacher, Ms. Smack. I recently visited Ms. Smack to talk about my old school. Other teachers including Ms. Derrickson, Ms. Chase, Ms. Holloway, Mr. Barnes, Ms. Harrell (White), Mr. Gatling, Ms. Robinson (Anderson), Ms. Fassett, Ms. Cornish, Ms. Nutter, Ms. Showell, and Mr. Pearson will always be remembered. Teachers in my family, Aunt Mildred Handy and Marie Connelly, my cousin, also made a big impression on me. They inspired me so early in life. Because of them, I thought I understood how to run the school—how everything was supposed to work. After all, I loved homework. I enjoyed helping my schoolmates. My mom encouraged me to continue listening to my teachers and to take advantage of everything I could learn. I had to because every day she would ask me what I had learned.

MY ELEMENTARY DISAPPOINTMENT

How could I be disappointed in this school? *No way this could happen.* I believe it happened when I started third grade. Looking for my friend on the first day, I became confused. I waited for him because I was sure we would be in the same class. After all, we rode the same school bus.

When my friend didn't arrive in my class, I decided to do something about it. I went across the hall to our second-grade class. I figured my friend might be mixed up. There he sat, at the same desk he sat in last year. I tried to encourage my friend to come with me. But he said *no.* I started pulling on his arm. He pulled back, then the teachers came.

No Albin, he must stay here for another year.
This is last year's class; he belongs with me in the third grade!

They wouldn't listen. They took me back to my class. I became so sad for my friend. I later learned that my friend needed to repeat the second grade. I tried to help him. I really did. I learned a valuable lesson. School was a place to learn. If you didn't take it seriously, you could be in school for a long time.

MY SCHOOL FRIENDS AT RECESS

Recess is something children always look forward to. Running, jumping, playing dodgeball with those stinging hard red balls or just enjoying being outdoors. We spent most of our recess challenging our classmates in racing competitions. Boys and girls would sprint down an open path between the buildings. I moved my short legs as fast as I could, but to no avail.

I experienced a few disappointments in racing that seemed to occur time after time. My cousin, Bernida Waples, and Vonda Briddell beat me—and all the boys in class—in races over and over again. I realized that I needed to get better at running. I also couldn't take anything away from those two girls. Vonda and Bernida were some of the most talented athletes in my grade.

The opportunity to get out of the classroom every day at recess was something we always looked forward to. We didn't have a lot, but we were happy just being outside together.

THE BIG BUILDING

It was an honor to be in the *Big Building;* once we were promoted to fourth grade, we earned that honor. It was one long structure with classrooms on both sides of the hallway. There was a sliding door between the two sixth grade classes. When that unique door was opened, there was one big classroom. It was also where Principal Spry's office was. I couldn't wait until I got into the Big Building.

My cousins would say, *You're going to love the Big Building.*

Jumping off the bus to find my new classroom on the first day of fourth grade excited me. The building housed fourth, fifth, and sixth graders. We could order these fantastic cheeseburgers for lunch. I will never forget those delicious cheeseburgers. I also loved the choices of ice cream. Fourth grade was the start of some wonderful memories…an experience interrupted by a mistake I made during that year.

Not one student in the school wanted to visit our principal, Ms. Spry. The loud whacks followed by crying discouraged everyone. You could hear what was happening in her office or another student would tell you. Mrs. Spry's paddle looked *so big*…almost too big to be picked up. I did visit her office once. That story started just after recess one day.

Our teacher said, *Go to the restroom before class starts.*

Almost the entire classroom of boys ended up in the restroom. There were too many boys in one place. Two of my classmates started pushing each other. Back and forth they went. It looked like a fight. They just kept walking around, shoulder to shoulder, waiting for the other to swing first. All the other boys just stood around watching.

I stepped up to say *Baddest man—hit my hand!*

To be fair, all the fights started this way. So, I was just following the unwritten protocol. One person would slap my hand first. I would then slap his opponent. This meant the guy who hit my hand hit the other guy, not me. This is how the fight started. The teachers rushed in to break up the fight.

They asked, *Who started the fight?*

All the boys pointed to me. They knew the protocol but singled me out anyway, so I had to visit Ms. Spry's office. I never knew it was such a long walk to her office. That day, every step I took made her office seem farther and farther away. I kept thinking about what I was going to say. When I reached her office, I had it figured out. I gazed over in the direction of her paddle in the corner. Ms. Spry said, *Explain to me what happened. Albin, tell me why you started the fight.* That day was the first time I spoke up for myself—the first time I really communicated like an adult or a lawyer. I think I proved my case by saying I never threw a punch. In fact, I told Mrs. Spry that I liked both guys involved in the fight. They also liked me.

> *I don't think you know, Ms. Spry, but fights in this school always start this way.*
> *What do you mean?*
> I explained the *baddest man protocol.*
> She then said, *Why did you feel you should be the person to start the fight?*
> *They were taking a long time to start. Plus, class would be starting soon.*
> She said, *Well, look at you. You're not in class now, are you?*

No, but I should be.

I don't want this to happen again. You understand?

Yes.

I got a strong warning: *Look at that paddle.*

I took a good look at her paddle. The more I looked at it, the bigger it got.

I think I got lucky…probably because I was the smallest kid in the class. Everyone in class looked at me expecting me to be crying when I walked through the door. I just returned to my desk and raised my hand to answer the first question I could. When they asked me what happened, I just said *No one can use the baddest man protocol anymore.* I discouraged anyone in my class from using the *baddest man protocol* whenever the situation called for me to do that. I would never visit her office again. Another lesson learned. I do not know if my mother ever found out about it. If she did, she never mentioned it.

CLASS DISCUSSION ABOUT THE GAME OF BASKETBALL

I know school is a place for learning, but basketball was on my mind all the time. As I mentioned before, my big brother Ronald played basketball. I admired his love for basketball. Let's face it—I liked everything about him…his confidence and just the way he carried himself.

One weekend, Ronald drove me to Germantown, a Black neighborhood in Berlin. His teammates put together some weekend basketball play. To my surprise, he pulled up to the house of my classmate, Ron Dixon. It was so good to see Ron outside of the classroom. His twin brothers Frankie and Calvin both played on Ronald's basketball team. I watched them run around the court that Saturday. Of course, they were playing on a *dirt* court. They played so hard against each other; I wasn't sure they were friends. On my way home, I couldn't stop thinking about that game. That day sealed my love for the game of basketball. To watch those high school players up close was amazing.

I was so glad to see Ron's interest in basketball, too. After all, both our brothers played on the same team. Our brothers played against other all-Black high school teams. I watched them play against high school teams that don't exist anymore because of integration—schools like Woodson High, Mace Lane High, Somerset High, Jason High, Moton High, and Salisbury High.

Sometimes I would have the opportunity to ride the bus to the game with my big sister— but only on Friday nights. I tried to get on the bus during a weeknight to go to the game. My Aunt HaHa would not let me go. I was so disappointed that I went to the bedroom and cried.

The games gave my classmate Ron and me something to talk about in school. I couldn't wait to see the basketball write-ups. I would bring the sports page that showed our game results to school the next day. For Worcester High, the Dixon brothers and Ronald were the scoring stars. My classmate and I enjoyed talking about the basketball game that occurred the night before.

CLASS COMPETITION

Have you ever heard of a class challenge organized by students without their teacher's knowledge? In the sixth grade, a group of students loved school so much that we did just that—created a challenge, a competition between the girls and the boys. It was just for fun not only during recess, but in the classroom, too. Which team would answer the most questions by the end of the day? I don't know where we got the girls vs. boys challenge from, but we sure enjoyed playing the game. We selected a scorekeeper for the boys and a scorekeeper for the girls. They were usually in the back of the class. For each correct answer, team points were awarded. I am not sure how long we played during the school year, but I do know that our class participation went way up. Everyone kept raising their hands whenever the teacher asked a question. Each team felt a sense of pride each day they won. We tried to hide what we were doing from our teachers. I sort of think the teachers knew what we were up to, but continued to let us play the game. The sixth-grade class competition was just another memorable fun experience we had at Flower Street Elementary.

AN HONOR TO BE A PATROLMAN

I prayed my teacher, Mr. Barnes, would give me the opportunity to be a patrolman. Being a patrolman was the biggest honor an elementary student could receive. I was thrilled to get that chance in the fifth grade. Words can't explain how inspired I felt. From what I remember, the program featured five officers: Sherwood Purnell, Milton Purnell, Oliver Purnell, Ron Dixon, and me. Sherwood and Milton became captains. Oliver, Ron, and I became lieutenants. There were many other students who became members of the patrolman club. However, only the five of us became officers.

A community school best describes Flower Street Elementary. Many students walked to school. Cars in the community stopped to allow students to cross the street. Our patrolman duties resembled those of today's crossing guards—we would assist our fellow students at crossings, before and after school. One of our responsibilities each morning was putting up the American Flag. At the end of the day, we took down the flag. We also learned to fold the flag. Each morning, several patrolmen held the doors to allow students to go to class. We did the same when the bell rang at the end of the day. We did this for safety reasons. We also helped the teachers when needed. It was truly an honor to be a patrolman at Flower Street Elementary School. I will always remember all the respect our fellow students and our teachers gave us, even in elementary school.

GRADUATION FROM FLOWER STREET ELEMENTARY

Leaving Flower Street Elementary—a school I fell in love with on Day One—was difficult. This was the only school I had ever been in. There were teachers who acted like our parents because they really cared about us. I spent six years at a school where I started in the first grade. Coming from the very small town of Bishop, I met so many lifelong friends. Now I would be entering a new school where I would have to meet new friends again. Our class prepared to go to Worcester High School, an all-Black school down in Newark, Maryland. The school bus ride would take almost an hour each way, but it was a school all my family members had attended.

My cousins said, *Albin, you're going to love Worcester High. You're going to have to run a mile every day in gym class, though. If you don't run fast enough, the gym teacher will make you pay.*

As a rising sixth grader, I was nervous hearing that.

CHAPTER 14

MY SPORTS DEVELOPMENT WITH LARRY, JUNIE & CHARLIE

As I got older, I began to hang out with my older cousins, Larry and John (Junie), and our friend Charlie. We did everything together, often challenging ourselves: two on two on the dirt basketball courts for hours; no equipment tackle football. Luckily, no one got seriously hurt. Again, two on two baseball—can you imagine trying to cover all the bases with a pitcher and one outfielder? At times we played with a real baseball; other times we used a rubber ball. Never having a real bat, swinging a stick or a tree branch was the best we could do.

When it came to basketball, we continued to put up our own basketball court. We designed the basketball court boundary lines. We did the same on our farmland fields to play baseball and football. We played just about every day after school. The weekends were reserved for all day play. Just about every time we competed, the same teams were formed. The teams would be Junie and Charlie vs. Larry and me. The games would end with Larry and Junie fighting. Charlie and I would just be sitting on the sideline watching. One thing was for sure we did not sit around in the house. Our parents demanded that we went outside.

CHAPTER 15

WHY I QUIT MY FIRST JOB IN OCEAN CITY, MARYLAND

When I was around thirteen years old, I no longer wanted to work in the hot sun. I didn't want to be in the blueberry field anymore. One of my best friends, Lonnie Mercer, and his brother, Donnie Mercer, started working in Ocean City. I wanted to work down in Ocean City along with them. After all, they were my next-door neighbors at the time. A gentleman by the name of Mr. Potlow, I believe, helped get us the jobs. Lonnie started working for the Delmarva Hotel. I landed a job working with Donnie at the Lackawanna Restaurant.

Neither of us had a means of transportation to come back to work each day. So, we got a room in Ocean City, about a block away from work. It only cost us $5.00 a day each for the room. The room, only about 10' x 10', wasn't much, but it saved us a lot of frustration about finding a ride to and from work. No one had a car. Lodging only a half block from the boardwalk, we spent a lot of time there. It was so much fun, but we were spending our money every night. The attractions, the games, popcorn, and french fries took almost all our money each week. Ocean City was a completely different world from our little town, Bishop. We should have been saving more.

We worked as dishwashers. Washing the silverware in this machine with very hot water became my main job. We always cleaned up the dishwashing area and mopped it before we left for the evening. One evening, we heard all this commotion coming from inside the restaurant. We rushed to look through the window, as we weren't allowed in the restaurant section. What we saw shocked both of us. We saw the owner yelling and cursing at this young man. As we looked closer, we could see that owner started punching this person over and over again. We then realized that the young man he continued to punch looked like his son…holding him and punching him like an adult. His son was about our age. It scared the heck out of us. The owner looked like he went crazy. What could his son have done that was so bad? I said to myself, *He's not going to do that to me.* He did not see us watching him through the window. We quickly finished cleaning up. Then we got out of there as fast as possible.

The owner always came in the back with a bad attitude, demanding things right away. He would say to me, *I need the silvers right now.* (He really meant he wanted the silverware right now.) I would rush to get it to him. It always upset me the way he talked down to us. One day he came in angrier than usual.

He looked at me and shouted, *Give me the silvers!*

Sweating to keep up, washing the silverware as fast as I could—frustrated, I looked up at him. *Here's your silvers!* I threw all of it on the counter. I walked out the back door of the restaurant. The door, only about ten steps away, seemed like twenty. As I walked toward the door, I prayed he wouldn't follow me. All I could think of was him coming after me, like he did his son. When I finally reached the door, I ran as fast as I could across the street. I raced to tell Lonnie, who worked down the street, that I quit. I called my mom to tell her that I quit.

She said, *Come on home, son.*

I went to the foot of the Rt. 50 bridge to thumb my way back home. I kept looking to see if the owner might come looking for me. I finally got a ride that took me so close to home that I could walk the rest of the way. I was relieved when I finally got there. My mother never wanted me to be away from home that young anyway.

CHAPTER 16

THE DECISION TO ATTEND STEPHEN DECATUR HIGH SCHOOL

At a time when segregation played a big part in our lives, we pondered the thought of making the big jump. Not knowing what to expect—just knowing it would be a new journey—we would be entering a different world: students speaking the same language, but being a different race. Our decision to become Stephen Decatur Seahawks or become Worcester High Indians wasn't easy. One consideration: most of my family graduated from Worcester High. I remember family members singing *Oh Worcester High,* their school song, for years. The lyrics will always be in my head. My cousins continued to tease me about how hard it would be in the physical education class. I think most of my cousins thought I would enroll in Worcester.

In the sixth grade, our class was set to go to Worcester High School. (This is where the Worcester County Board of Education is housed today.) We received information to take home that read: *In a few years, all the schools in Worcester County are going to be integrated. So, here is your opportunity to attend Stephen Decatur early.* Our parents would have to sign the permission slip. Most of my class went on to Worcester High, the only all Black high school in the county. A few of my friends and I, including Oliver Purnell and Ron Dixon, decided to go to Decatur. I was influenced by my cousin, Larry Waples, the first African American who attended Decatur the year before, all by himself. He kind of opened the door and we just walked through. History will show him being the first African American to integrate the school and maybe the county. It's hard to imagine him walking the halls for an entire year, all by himself. Back then the grades at Decatur were 7th – 12th. After a few days of making the adjustments of coming from a school with all Black teachers and going to a school with all White teachers, I started to have some doubts. You see, I almost never got to see my friends until the bell rang at the end of the day. At times that made me feel like I was in the school by myself. Because I was so short as a 7th grader, when I walked the halls, everyone seemed so tall and I felt a bit lost.

So, I got my nerve up one morning while waiting for the school bus. I told my mom I wasn't sure if I had made the right decision to go to Decatur. She never asked me why.

> Without hesitation Mom asked, *Do you remember when you brought that paper home— and I asked you if you were sure before I signed it? Yes, I remember.*
> *Well, son you made a commitment to that school, and you must honor that commitment.*
> *Okay.*
> She said, *Well I will see you tonight; your lunch is on the table.*

We never had that conversation again. But I could see her watching me leave on the bus every day. Later she told me that she cried every morning for the first three months. *And* that she prayed every day for my safe return each evening.

You see, by the time I graduated my experience was most gratifying. Oh, I was still shorter than almost everyone. However, I could find my classes with my eyes closed. I had made so many lifelong friends. Although my teachers were strict, they had become almost like parents. I had the opportunity to play four different sports and bring home the only Maryland State Basketball Championship in the school's history. Earlier I mentioned my schoolmates, Oliver Purnell and Ron Dixon. We were the starting guards for our state championship team.

I fell in love with Stephen Decatur High School early, even when some of my friends questioned my choice. I felt good about my choice after the conversation with my mother. After all, Flower Street Elementary prepared me well. I felt very comfortable in the classroom. I wanted to learn as much as possible because my mother wanted me to. I also discovered the school's basketball team and knew we had to earn good grades to play. I put a priority on my studies to make sure my grades would be good. Sports teams at the school interested me, especially basketball.

Coach was able to find the 7th and 8th graders a couple games to play, but for the most part we were managers. We couldn't try out for the junior varsity team until the 9th grade. This allowed us to be in the gym to watch the players. We got the chance to learn from the players. We also got a chance to practice ourselves, on a real gym floor. Having only played on dirt courts, we were in heaven. After school, we hustled to be the first players in the gym. That way we could get some shots up before practice started.

This was a time when there were many changes in our lives. History was in the making, but we didn't realize it at first. There was the first African American to attend Stephen Decatur in Larry. Larson Jarman became the first African American on the basketball team to earn a sports letter in basketball. Then came something unbelievable that still to this day puts a smile on my face...the first time a school day had been named for a student; it was named for an African American, Cliff Small. Small made the game-winning shot to beat Wicomico High School. This was the first time in the school's history that the Seahawks won against Wicomico High. It was unbelievable when the principal made the announcement. It came across the intercom loud and clear. He said, *Today is Cliff Small Day.* Sitting at my homeroom desk I felt so proud. I couldn't wait to see him walking down the hall so I could congratulate him. He couldn't be any happier than I was about his honor. My love for Decatur started increasing every day.

I did have one concern. My community friends didn't like the fact that I enrolled at Decatur early. All the friends who lived around me enrolled at a Black high school…me attending a White school didn't sit well with some at first. However, a couple years later they also enrolled at Decatur. Schools had been segregated for years; now it was almost time to integrate.

CHAPTER 17

MY OPPORTUNITY TO PLAY ON THE TEAM

Basketball motivated me to do many positive things in my life such as reading my first sports book, *Go Up for Glory,* by the Hall of Famer—the great Boston Celtic Bill Russell. Since Bill Russell's teammate John Hondo Havlicek was my favorite player, it made me more interested in reading the book, an intriguing read that I review even today. I believe without sports, I wouldn't be where I am today. For me—understanding discipline, teamwork, and the value of a good attitude all came from basketball. I learned how important hitting the books can be in determining your future. I devoted a lot of time to studying. At times I completed homework with the help of only dim lights in our house. Because basketball took up a lot of time, finding time to study often became difficult. The team sometimes got the opportunity to do our homework after school in study hall. This time was valuable since getting homework done helped me maintain good grades, which allowed me to be a team manager. Keeping good grades prepared me for the day when I would be allowed to play on the Seahawks Junior Varsity team. Because of sports, I learned good study habits. I enjoyed establishing good relationships with my teachers. Through sports, I became motivated to do better in the classroom. I wanted to represent my school on the court *and* off the court. I didn't want to be a student who failed the team by failing in school.

If I wanted to play basketball, I needed to put in a lot of work. In the eighth grade, I watched our varsity team continue to get better. They practiced hard every night. As a manager, I tried to learn everything I could, keeping in mind that the next year I would get my opportunity to play. I took advantage of learning from players like Cliff Small, Bill Gibbs, Larsen Jarmon, Bobby Baker, Jerry Todd, Vaugh White, Grover Collins, Bob Connors, David Pitts, and Larry Hobbs.

I worked out on my own, using the same drills our team used: Jumping, lay-up drills, free throw shooting, dribbling, defensive slides, line runs, and jump shots. I watched players every day. I focused on playing basketball as much as possible outside or inside—it didn't matter. I just wanted to be in the best shape possible.

I remember getting up one Saturday and calling my father. He lived in Berlin, about ten miles away. I told him I was on my way down. Little did he know I was going to run every step of the way. Never had I challenged myself with such a long run, but that day I wanted to prove to myself that I could do it.

During that time in my life, we didn't have a car. All my friends and I walked or hitch-hiked a ride to wherever we wanted to go. Not this time. The skies were blue and sunny, and there was no wind that day. As I started my light jog, I began to make landmark goals. My first landmarks were my two friends' houses. Next, I wanted to make it the Bill Lewis Gas Station. The more landmarks I reached, the more confident I got that I could make it. The landmarks were key to me reaching my father's house. People kept stopping to see if I wanted a ride. I would say, *No, I am running down to my father's house.* When I finally arrived at my father's house, he asked me,

How did you get here?
I ran, Dad.
You're kidding!

He couldn't believe it. After an hour or two of spending time with my brothers, it was time to head back home. But first I called my mother to tell her I was on my way back. I started my run back doing the same thing I had done on my run to father's—looking for landmarks. I was determined to make it, although the sweat poured down my face. As I approached the small town called Showell, there was no stopping me. Every time I felt myself getting fatigued, I tried to relax. I tried to breathe normally. When I could see my mother's house, I became a bit overwhelmed—so excited I started to sprint! Happy that I accomplished my self-challenge, I finished like I was racing someone else. I didn't realize it at the time, but I made the ten-mile run back without a drop of water. I cherished the fact that I did it without stopping. My legs still felt strong, which made me feel good. Although I only weighed 135 pounds, I felt I was in the best shape ever.

However, it didn't seem like it at the end of the first night's basket-ball tryouts. Coach Ward Lambert made us run wind sprints at the end of practice. I gave it all I could because I wanted to win each time. When his whistle blew, getting a jump on everyone seemed to be the key. The wind sprints hurt so bad, they almost made me feel like quitting. I felt like I couldn't move anymore. All the players collapsed on the floor before we mustered enough energy to get up just to do everything all over again…not an easy pre-season training session at all. It was like my distance running never helped. My heart pumped so fast. Coach's suicide sprints, as they were sometimes called, became a different kind of training. He looked for players who were hustling for every loose ball. The box out drills deter-mined who really wanted the basketball. It was important to me to show the coach how much I wanted to make the team. It was a dream of mine.

There were a couple problems that I needed to correct. When I drib-bled, I would run past the ball. Can you imagine dribbling with the ball behind you? I couldn't figure out how to keep the ball in front of me.

Coach said, *I want you to practice pushing the ball out in front of you when you dribble.* After all my hard work, my legs started to hurt. The pain came from my shins. A severe case of shin splints caused me to sit out a few drills. It seemed that my flat feet caused the pain, but I couldn't stop if I wanted to make the team.

Basketball tryouts were finally over. It was time to find out if all my hard work had paid off. Coach said, *The names of the players who made the Junior Varsity and Varsity will be posted on the wall in the gymnasium tomorrow morning.* I prayed I would make Junior Varsity.

My mom said, *Don't worry so much about it. As long as you did your best, just go to sleep.* But I couldn't sleep—all night! All I could think of on the ride to school was that list of names. When my bus arrived at school, I couldn't wait. I jumped off the bus, raced in the front doors, and sprinted down to the gym. I stopped to say one last prayer before I opened the gym doors. I slowly opened the door—no one was in there. I walked to the gym wall and read the Varsity list first. My name did not appear on that list, but when I saw my name on the Junior Varsity list, I wanted to call my mom right away.

My coach, Dick Burbage, encouraged me to play with a lot of passion. He had watched me hanging around the gym for a couple years. He said, *I want you to put your heart in the game.* His pep talks motivated me. He didn't seem to care that I stood just over 5'. I didn't care either. He taught me how to guard any opponent—even if they were taller than me. My goal was to take the ball away from my opponent using my speed and agility.

I became too competitive. I didn't want to come out of the practice scrimmages or games. I remember expressing that one night during a game. I took my uniform off, acting like I quit. Disgusted about being taken out of the game, I wasn't thinking about my teammates who hadn't gotten a chance to play. I am so glad Coach Burbage gave me another chance.

Going into my sophomore year, I worked hard at basketball skills all summer. I trained every day. I even wore leg weights while I was competing against good ball players on the Fourth Street Basketball Courts in Ocean City, Maryland. Any day of the week you could find a mixture of high school, college, and sometimes pro ball players on the court. Every day, something new could be learned. I tried to soak it all in.

In the tenth grade, I hoped to play on the Varsity team. I wanted to play with my Flower Street Elementary schoolmates. Oliver, Ron, Milton, and Sherwood Purnell all made Varsity. However, I was back on Junior Varsity for another year. I would have to wait to play with them for another year, or so I thought. It was a blessing because I went on to break the JV scoring record with 36 points in one game. The record of 29 points was established by my cousin Milton Purnell the year before.

Our Varsity team was good all season that year—District Champs, Regional Champs…heading to States at the University of Maryland College Park for the first time. To my surprise, Coach Lambert said, *I am moving you, Lonnie, and Mike Parker up to Varsity at the end of the JV season.* I was so happy even though we were not expected to play. However, I did get the opportunity to play a few minutes during the Districts and the Regional games. I was so excited, but nervous! At States, we won the first game in the semi-finals, then got beat in the championship game by Fairmont Heights High School. It was a sad time for our team, after going undefeated all season. We had a very quiet ride back home as we reflected on our loss, but I knew we would be back the next year. Our slogan would become *Victory is always sweeter after first tasting defeat.*

On my first visit to College Park, our team finished second in the state of Maryland. I learned so much from watching the seniors—Larry Hobbs, Grover Collins, Richard Jackson, and Jim Farlow.

CHAPTER 18

THE ROAD TO THE MARYLAND STATE CHAMPIONSHIP

I took the loss of that state championship game personally; I was devastated. I knew that it was a team effort, and the loss was a team loss. I could still see the sadness on the faces of our players—the feeling we had after suffering the loss compared to the feeling we had at the start of the game. But I also remembered the thrill of getting to that championship game. I wanted to have that feeling not just for me, but for my coach, my teammates, our school, and our community. We hadn't achieved what we had set out to do. I believed that we could return to the University of Maryland, but this time with a different outcome. So, what did I need to do as an individual to help make that happen?

I decided that I needed to get better at the game. What should I do? There were no summer leagues or summer camps where I lived. The first thing I needed to do after my sophomore season was to look for a basketball camp. I needed to improve my skills going into my junior season. My teammate Robert Mumford and I decided to attend the *Jack Kraft Villanova Basketball Camp* in Greenland, Pennsylvania. Kraft, the head basketball coach at Villanova University, operated a good camp. We were so excited to meet his players, Chris Ford, Howard Porter, and Tom Ingelsby. They were our coaches for the week. The experience we had exceeded our expectations. We stayed in military style sleeping facilities with about forty bunk beds in each building. We were up nearly every morning for breakfast at the cafeteria.

Then warm-ups, stretching, running, defensive drills, then lunch. I remembered standing in a single line hoping to get a chance to make a call home: only one pay phone in our area for almost forty players. Each afternoon saw offensive drills, team practices, team games, then dinner, film watching, and more team games. We played on outdoor basketball courts—no indoor courts.

Robert and I both learned a lot at camp and that's what we were there for. The one thing that stuck in my head from that camp was how to use your abilities on the defensive side of the ball. When the basketball leaves a player's hand as he dribbles, it is no longer in his control. That means the ball is as good yours as it is his. Consequently, I worked on the technique of stealing the ball every practice.

I made some wonderful friends, but I didn't think I'd ever see them again. During my senior year, Villanova reached the NCAA Final Four. They ended up losing to John Wooden's UCLA team, 68-62. I was pulling for the players I had met at camp.

I got my first basketball scholarship offer from Elmira College in Elmira, New York. I don't know why I didn't accept the offer right on the spot, but the coach gave me a year to decide. Now that I reflect, I wonder what I was thinking. Elmira was an all-girls school and in two years it was going co-ed. It would soon have its first men's basketball program. What an opportunity that would have been in many ways! My cousin John "Junie" Jones was so excited. He bragged about the offer to all his friends. He would say, *Did you hear my cousin got a basketball scholarship offer in New York?*

MY FIRST CAR

Going into my junior year of high school I wanted a car, but first I needed to get my license. I needed my license to travel different places to play basketball and go to school. It was time for me to stop using my hitchhiking thumb to get everywhere. During that summer, I practiced parking with good friend Earl Timmons. He already had a car and his license. I had turned sixteen and Earl, who I called Beaver, picked me up from school and took me to try to get my license. I was so nervous when taking my driving test and even more nervous when it came to parking. When the instructor said I passed, I almost fainted. I was so overjoyed that I asked Beaver if I could drive back to school. I couldn't wait to tell my friends!

Having my license allowed me to say to my father that I needed a car to drive to school. He said, *You will have to work for it this summer. I will check around for you.* Little did I know, the car he would select would be right behind our house. *Mr. Herb will sell you his car for $100.*

I looked at the car, a 1962 Chevy II Nova. I told my father that I didn't want that car; I wanted a better car. I could see the car out my bedroom window. After a few days of looking at the car, I told my father that I wanted it. I bought the car and drove it less than 200 feet to our yard.

My father said, *You know you must get the car inspected and get insurance on it for a year.*
For a year?! School is not even open a whole year!

I worked all summer to get the car inspected and to get insurance. I cleaned and polished the car every day, anticipating the first day of school. I even brought some moon hubcaps that really shined.

Then came the first day of school. I came to school early and parked in the front row, right in front of the gymnasium. I wanted all the students to see my car. Students were walking by saying,

Hondo has a car!
In my mind, I was saying, *Yep, Hondo has a car!*

I was so proud of my car. I decided it was almost time for the bell to ring. Just as I was about to get out of my car, someone parked next to me. Now I thought my car was clean, polished, and looking good. When I looked at the car beside me, I could see that the driver was one of my classmates, Leighton Moore. He was getting out of a beautiful brand-new orange Corvette. As Leighton was getting out, I started slouching down in my car. I didn't want him to see me. How embarrassing.

MY FIRST GOAL

Setting goals in high school, especially for basketball, kept me thinking positive. Before my junior school year, we played basketball everywhere. I had one goal in mind: make the varsity team. In my junior year tryouts, I gave it all I could. I prayed the night before teams were to be announced. I got off the bus and raced down to the gym to see if I had made varsity and there it was. I had achieved my first goal of the season. I had made it to the varsity team, probably the smallest player at 5'5" to ever make the cut. I felt I had a chance to make the team because of my speed. But I still had some doubt. My mother said, *Don't worry, you are a lucky kid.*

When asked about me, Head Coach Ward Lambert said, *Hondo more than makes up for his lack of height by his quickness; he is the fastest player on the team.*

I loved concentrating on harassing my opponent on defense. Most players liked to score baskets. I liked to figure out their weaknesses and take advantage of them on defense. I knew that the ball was on the floor as much as it was in the air. This gave me a chance to make a steal off a dribble, make a deflection or intercept a pass.

On offense for the past two years, I had learned to shoot jump shots. Coach asked us to locate our favorite spot on the court to shoot from. After putting up many shot attempts all over the court I made my decision. I settled for an area on the right side of the free throw line, known as the elbow by players. I took most of my shots from that area before practice. I needed to learn to dribble better and become a better passer. On offense, I used my speed to beat my opponent down the court for easy baskets. Speed became an asset for me. One of my teammates, Brazil Briddell, said, *Hondo was fast. Starting on the baseline, Oliver would throw the ball down the court. Hondo would always beat the ball to the other end of the court.*

MY SECOND GOAL

A very important step in a player's career is to become a starter on the team. All the training wasn't just to make the team; I had another goal in mind. My second goal for the season was to be a starter with my friends, Oliver and Ron. Milton and Sherwood, two other graduates from Flower Street Elementary School, were already starters. I worked hard during the practices, hustling on defense and offense. I may not have been a big rebounder, but I tried to make up for it by winning every suicide line run. As a point guard, I would give up my good shot for a teammate's better shot.

I guess I was lucky to be on the team with such a great group of guys. My teammates were so talented that there was no time to take off a play—not even in practice or during scrimmage games. Coach Lambert's team managers were very dedicated to him. They were the most important people on the team besides the players. The managers sat in the bleachers to take notes. Coach would have them give the players points, both negative and positive points. Obviously, we were very kind to the managers.

The goal was to have as many positive points as possible. Coach would post the tallied scores from the highest to the lowest each morning. The top five players would be the starters, either in practice or in the next game. No player liked practice because coach was so hard on us, but no player missed practice either.

MY THIRD GOAL

Our team goal was to get back to College Park and this time to win. The first step was to advance through the districts. Two victories later and we could be State Champs. Coach Lambert used a 3-1-1 defensive press on defense. This type of defense was designed to put pressure on our opponents. The press forced turnovers, double dribbles, and bad passes. He challenged us every day to run the press to perfection. If we didn't run the press correctly, suicide sprints would be next. We practiced our free throws when we were exhausted. This made it much more like a game-type situation. Box-out drills were performed as if in a real game. We dove for loose balls because our coach wanted 100% effort. Our team practiced shooting every day to improve efficiency. But our defense allowed us to make easy layup baskets. We did pre-season scrimmages, mainly against Delaware schools, to see how our defense looked.

Our team was starting to come together. The talent levels on our team were very close. In practice, our starting five team often lost to our second five. The second five often lost to the third five during practice. That's why our players couldn't take any plays off. We were encouraged to hustle on every play in practice.

PLAYING FOR THE SCHOOL AND THE COMMUNITY

Playing in front of a jam-packed crowd at the University of Maryland Eastern Shore, we lost by two points to Washington High School. We were undefeated until this blemish on our record.

We were disappointed at the outcome, feeling like our hopes and dreams of reaching College Park again might not happen. Our hopes of bringing back the State Basketball Championship might not happen. We had just lost a game to a team that we had beat earlier by two points. This time they were the ones rejoicing with a two-point victory.

I was devastated that night until my coach came into the locker room. We were sitting in there in a state of shock, with our confidence shaken. Some of my teammates were crying, while others were feeling we had just let our community down. The thought of the anticipated tongue lashing we were going to get from Coach made us feel worse.

When our coach entered the room, he stopped and said, *This loss has just made us Maryland State Champions.* We were confused at first, because how could a loss make us state champions? We didn't know it then, but it was another one of his motivational speeches. Maybe the stiff competition we faced that night was his reason for saying that. Anyway, six games later, we were celebrating after being crowned Maryland State Basketball Champions in College Park on the campus of the University of Maryland. How did Coach know?

My junior year became the best basketball year in our school's history with that victory. Little did we know that it would be the best for the next 50 years. No basketball team from our school has ever won another state championship since. We were a proud and close team, probably because 13 of the 15 players graduated from Flower Street Elementary. Some of us had been in school together for 12 years. All of us started our basketball playing careers on outside dirt courts. The championship was important because it was the last year before schools were going to be integrated. Our team was well-prepared because of all the blood, sweat and tears we shared during practices. We didn't realize it at first, but our team was sort of making history. Our team was starting to bring our community together. How might you ask? Blacks and Whites were talking to each other. Our team created a buzz among our citizens. Blacks and Whites even started to come to the games together and sitting next to each other. More and more people started coming to the games. Throughout that season, our gymnasium was full for every home game. People who didn't get into the gym wouldn't leave. Some were allowed in a room to watch the game on the television. Others just stood outside, hoping to get scores after each quarter. A couple times before the game started, I almost didn't get in.

One of Coach Lambert's motivational techniques was the team showcase displayed in the hallway, directly in our view as we arrived in the building each morning. I visited that showcase every day during the season—sometimes two or three times during the day. We were so proud of that showcase. Many students also visited our display during the school day. Our pep rallies kept us excited about our teams. Coach posted the scores from each game and our records to date. For instance, the first game read 1-0 and 21 to go, SD 80 James M. Bennett 49. It was very important that we were still playing when the board read *1 to go*, because that meant we were in the state championship.

Below are the final results posted on the Seahawks Basketball Team showcase:

STEPHEN DECATUR BASKETBALL ROAD TO THE CHAMPIONSHIP

1 and 0 and 21 to go:	SD 80 James M. Bennett 49
2 and 0 and 20 to go:	SD 78 Crisfield 51
3 and 0 and 19 to go:	SD 132 Alumni 45
4 and 0 and 18 to go:	SD 108 Snow Hill 31
5 and 0 and 17 to go:	SD 76 Pocomoke 38
6 and 0 and 16 to go:	SD 77 Wi Hi 43
7 and 0 and 15 to go:	SD 93 Worcester 52
8 and 0 and 14 to go:	SD 102 Colonel Richardson 42
9 and 0 and 13 to go:	SD 52 Washington 50
10 and 0 and 12 to go:	SD 69 Pocomoke 56
11 and 0 and 11 to go:	SD 96 Snow Hill 28
12 and 0 and 10 to go:	SD 93 Wi Hi 72
13 and 0 and 9 to go:	SD 69 Crisfield 35
14 and 0 and 8 to go:	SD 99 Worcester 59
15 and 0 and 7 to go:	SD 92 Easton 38
16 and 1 and 6 to go:	SD 64 Washington 66
17 and 1 and 5 to go:	SD 93 James M. Bennett 55
18 and 1 and 4 to go:	SD 94 Easton 57
19 and 1 and 3 to go:	SD 79 Cambridge 59
20 and 1 and 2 to go:	SD 79 North Caroline 57
Maryland State Championship Semi-Finals	
21 and 1 and 1 to go:	SD 81 Harve de Grace 50
Maryland State Championship Finals	
22 and 1 and 0 to go:	SD 64 Frederick 63

SEMI-FINAL CHAMPIONSHIP GAME

The Maryland Coast Press reported that the Stephen Decatur Seahawks scored an easy win over the generally tough Havre de Grace Warriors. After a 44-18 half-time lead, the score reached 68-33—and Coach Lambert pulled many of his starters. With a roster of second stringers from the bench, the Seahawks still ended the rout with a commanding 31-point lead. The score of the semi-final's game stood at an overwhelming 81-50, in favor of the Seahawks.

We were one step from our goal of avenging our loss the year before in the state finals at the University of Maryland…twenty-four hours until our championship contest with the Frederick High Cadets.

CHAMPIONSHIP GAME

Here we were again. For the second straight year, we would be playing for the Maryland State Championship. Our finals opponent was Frederick High a team with a 22-game winning streak. As I look back, we were tested early, and we were forced to get out of our normal full court press defense. We were tied at the end of the first quarter, 22-22, but the second quarter saw Frederick race out to a 9-point lead. With defense adjustments, we came back to only trail 41-40 at the half. Frederick continued to lead 51-49 as the third quarter buzzer sounded. This was a close game until the final horn would sound.

We were trailing 61-60 with only 40 seconds remaining. Our teammate Marvin Small picked up a loose ball following a missed shot and made a 10-foot basket that put us up 62-61. Twenty-five seconds later, Milton Purnell clinched the victory with two free throws, making the score 64-61. Frederick scored a basket as time wound down to make the final score 64-63.

I can't explain the feeling of seeing those last seconds tick off. All the hard work we had put in had paid off. Our dedication was all worth it. We proved that Eastern Shore basketball could compete with teams across the bridge. So exhausted, I could barely join in with the celebration on the court. I was so happy. Throughout all the jumping and cheering, it really didn't sink in right away. In our locker room, I realized we were the best in the state. Little Berlin was the home of the Maryland State Basketball Champions.

A few years ago, I had the pleasure of meeting some of the players and the coach from the 1971 football team from T. C. Williams High School in Alexandria, Virginia. They were keynote speakers at our Mid-Atlantic Recreation & Parks Sports Alliance. The movie *Remember the Titans* was about their football team's journey.

As these nice gentlemen shared their story, I sat there just a few feet from them and couldn't help but think of our basketball team. Our story mirrors the *Remember the Titans* story. Our team brought Berlin and Ocean City together during a time when schools in our area were still segregated. Blacks and Whites talking about their team, sitting together at the games, cheering together, and traveling to the games together. In 1970, our citizens were proud to be associated with our team one year before our school was officially integrated in 1971. I truly believe a movie script could have been written.

An article in the Maryland Coast Press read:

Approximately 350 excited fans turned out last Sunday for an impromptu welcome home to the victorious Stephen Decatur Seahawks, who became the Maryland State Basketball Champions by wiping Frederick High 64 to 63 in the tournament finals.

Many of the well-wishers waited for about an hour to see their team escorted into Stephen Decatur parking lot by a contingent of two Ocean City fire trucks, one driven by Chief Roland "Fish" Powell himself.

The school colors were woven into a blue and white "Victory" sign placed on the roof over the main entrance to the school. Many of the fans had signs of their own creation to express the dominance of their champions.

The bus carrying the Seahawks was surrounded by the cheering jubilant crowd as it came to a stop. The team emerged carrying its victory trophy and the crowd broke into a "We're Number One" chant.

There were many articles about our championship weekend from the Maryland Coast Press. Some of the articles' headlines were:

Stephen Decatur Seahawks win State Basketball Champion, 64-63
Dixon Leads in Point Average
Foul Shots Help Champions Hawks
81-50 Win Led to Title Shot
Cheering Crowd Greets Seahawks
Another article from the Maryland Coast Dispatch stated,
Seahawks Won State Basketball Champion.

The part of the article that I will always remember stated, *In the game of giants, the race for the title was decided by the little men. Most troublesome of the Frederick Cadets was 5'5" Spencer Johnson who began by penetrating the Seahawks defense like it were a sieve. To halt Johnson and the cadet attack, Coach Ward Lambert went to a zone defense and inserted Decatur's 5'5" Albin Handy. Supposedly on the injured list, Handy covered Johnson like a cat. So successfully did Handy cover Johnson that the usually high scorer was held scoreless. Two days earlier, he scored 22 points in the Cadets semifinal victory over the Sherwood Warriors. At the game's end, Handy while jubilant could hardly carry himself off the floor. Throughout the celebration that followed the clinching of the title, the little defensive star sat quietly on the bench, only able to smile his happiness. Top scorer for the Seahawks was 5'8" Ronald Dixon with a total of 19 points to his credit. Nine baskets were made by Dixon and one foul shot. Second in scoring was Oliver Purnell who was also a tiger on defense. Purnell made five goals plus seven foul shots for a total of 17 points.*

Our team was really respected by the entire community. Principal Gladys Burbage was so proud and trusting of our team. I remember when something challenging happened at school one afternoon. Many students became very upset. They decided to protest by doing a sit-down in front of the cafeteria. None of those students were going to class. When the teachers could not get the students to go, members of our team were asked to help. Since we were so well-liked, we were able to encourage the students to go back to class. One by one, they got up and returned. Problem solved.

My junior year was a bittersweet year. We finally won the state championship, but in doing so, we lost our coach. He got the opportunity to coach in college. He became the new head basketball coach for then Salisbury State College, now Salisbury University. I became upset, but I understood. Because of our championship win, he became a sought-after coach. My teammates Larry Waples, Oliver Purnell, Ron Dixon, Sherwood Purnell, Milton Purnell, Marvin Small, Lonnie Mercer, Larry Duffy, Fason Purnell, Alfred Harrison, Rodney Tingle, Richard Hoskins, Mike Parker, and Joe Sturgis became my school brothers. Remember the patrolman officers for Flower Street Elementary School, Sherwood, Milton, Oliver, Ron and myself? We were the starting five for the State Championship team and 13 out of 15 players were patrolman at Flower Street Elementary.

Our cheerleaders became our biggest supporters. Faith Purnell, Linda Purnell, Jane Ferguson, Gretchen Plate, Susan Quillen, Carol Blankfard, Cathy Darnley, Susan Jackson, Shelia Davis, Sharrye Lyons, and Sandy Coates played a pivotal role in our success. For that I am so thankful to them. It was so inspiring to see some of the cheerleaders at our recent high school's 50th year reunion.

CHAPTER 19

NEW COACH FOR MY SENIOR YEAR

During the summer before senior year, we knew our basketball team would have a new coach. We had no clue who the coach might be. We assumed we would find out when school started.

I think I was the first team member to find out who our new coach was going to be. I met him in the gymnasium at City Hall in Ocean City, Maryland. Of all places, this is where I would start my professional career. Who knew? I was there shooting baskets and a gentleman came up to me and asked,

> *Are you Hondo?*
> *Yes, I am.*
> *I'm Howard Reynolds. I will be your new basketball coach at Stephen Decatur.*
> *Nice to meet you, Coach Reynolds.*

Coach Reynolds shared that he was from the Cumberland, Maryland area near Frostburg University. I enjoyed our conversation that day. I liked him from Day One. His goal was to get our team back to the University of Maryland to win another state championship—I liked that.

Our team practices were intense, challenging, and competitive. He brought something new to our practices: he implemented a slow-down passing offense. The results showed in our first game as we defeated James M. Bennett High School. The next day, the Daily Times sports headline read,

The Stephen Decatur High Seahawks will be tough to handle again this season.

This fact was so evident last night when the State Class B Champions ran roughshod over James M. Bennett here, 96-65.

We went on to have another historic regular season led by our returning starters: Ron, Oliver and myself. Other starters were Marvin Small, his brothers Melvin Small and Alfonso Small, and Terry Jacobs.

One of my greatest memories in qualifying for states happened at the Wicomico Youth & Civic Center. My cousin Linda Purnell and her sisters Wanda and Marie came to watch the game. I believe we were playing Cambridge High. Linda said,

Time was winding down at halftime. As the seconds ticked away, Albin dribbled the ball up the court, took a half-court shot, and it went in! We were so excited to see our cousin make such a big shot. We were jumping up and down, clapping. We were so happy!

I was so shocked to hear that they were at the game. Linda never told me they were there until many years later. I remember that shot. But when we ran to the locker room, the coach never mentioned it. He just started talking about our need to play better defense.

Our team went on to reach the championship game at Cole Field House; this time we lost. Over three years, we had a great run going—60 wins and 5 losses, winning the Maryland State Championship and two state championship runner-up finishes.

One local newspaper selected me to the All-District Team. I was so proud of the selection, as there were so many good players on the Eastern Shore of Maryland. I thought back to how it all started with me shooting in the dark by our dim porch light. I was honored because my teammates Oliver and Ron were also selected. Three players from the same team… this doesn't usually happen.

The write-up stated:

Albin Handy, at 5'5", is the shortest member on the entire squad, but probably the fastest. The hustling senior is the third member to be picked from the Decatur squad. Handy, another fine ball handler, could hit the outside shot or could drive, even though he was the shortest high school player in the District. Another demon on defense, Handy accounted for numerous intercepted passes and steals over the season.

Coach Reynolds was also our coach for baseball—a sport that Ron, Oliver, and I loved. Baseball was as popular in our area as basketball—probably because in our early days, there was a baseball league comprised of all African Americans. There were teams from towns like Berlin, Salisbury, Snow Hill, Princess Anne, as well as teams from Delaware and Virginia. There were baseball fields everywhere. We were influenced by all our fathers and family members playing.

If we were not playing basketball, we were playing baseball. We played everywhere we could. Many times, we didn't have real bases. We used anything to substitute for bases. We made a field next to my house. I was usually the smallest player, so I grew to become the designated pitcher. My pitching days ended when a line drive hit me between the eyes, knocking me out. I never saw that ball leave the bat. Once I came to, my outfield career began. I never came anywhere near the infield again.

We played in the sand holes of Berlin. One Saturday when I was spending the night with my good friend Ron, we decided to play baseball. A makeshift baseball field was in one of the many sand holes in the area. I can't remember who was pitching. I do know it wasn't me. Joe (Bull) Sturgis hit a ball so far that it went out of the sand hole. We raced to the top of the sand hole to search for the ball—and there it was. The ball landed in a farmer's pig pen. Next to the ball was a bloody pig. Joe, who was much stronger than any of us, had hit the ball so hard that it killed the pig. We were so afraid that we got out of there as fast as possible.

When I reached high school, center field became my position. My senior year, our team proved to be pretty good. When we beat Wicomico

High School for the first time, we made history at school. In the last inning, I reached first base on a bunt. I then stole second and third bases. I scored on a squeeze bunt by my good friend Herman Hickman. It was a thrilling victory…one for the books for our school. I never got the Hondo Handy School Day, but it was a good day.

After a great season, Coach took us on our first official visit to spend time with the Frostburg State University Bobcats. After arriving in Frostburg, we stopped to visit the head baseball coach. Then we were off to the campus where we were each paired with some athletes for the weekend. Little did we know, they were football players. Those guys told us about bobcats that ran around on the campus. That story convinced me. That night I knew I wasn't going to Frostburg. I couldn't stop thinking about those bobcats all night. I did learn later that it wasn't true. However, for me the damage was already done.

AWARDS BANQUET

At our Senior Athletic Sports Banquet, to my surprise, the guest speaker was none other than my old coach, Ward Lambert. He was the head basketball coach at Salisbury State College.

Coach Lambert announced that I was being honored as the year's outstanding senior athlete for Decatur. I couldn't believe it. I was sitting next to some of the best athletes in the school and my name was called. To top things off, I was also named the most valuable player for soccer. Coach Lambert shared this in his speech.

> Hondo is an example of someone who wanted something bad enough, went after it, and accomplished his goal. Handy was only 5' when he started playing basketball for Decatur, but he loved the game and showed that what counts is inside the heart.

He discussed an attitude that exemplifies a winning team in his speech. Mr. Lambert associated our reversal with the good attitudes the players always displayed, their willingness to practice, take advice, and play as a team.

> *Four years ago, the team had an 8-12 win-loss record. In the past three years, they have been state champions once and runner up twice.*
>
> *A player like Albin Handy shows how a winning attitude can overcome obvious shortcomings. Although much shorter than the average basketball player, Albin developed into a first-rate player because he had the desire.*

Following his speech, I knew I would be attending Salisbury State College. I called Coach Lambert and asked him if he thought I could play basketball at Salisbury. He said, *Hondo, if you think you can, you can.*

That was all the inspiration I needed. I just had to have the faith, the desire, and the determination to make my dream a reality.

CHAPTER 20
A NEW CHALLENGE AT SALISBURY STATE COLLEGE

Both dreams for the little boy from Bishop had started to come true in less than twenty-four hours. I had promised my mother since I was a young man that I was going to graduate from high school, then go to college, get that four-year degree, and be the first in my family to do so.

The night before your high school graduation, you might think about celebrating more than one night. You probably plan on getting together with your friends the next couple days. But not me and my teammate Ron Dixon. The excitement of our graduation at 8:00 p.m. was short lived. That next morning at 8:00 a.m. we were in our first college class. It was at that moment we knew our lives were changing. In just over twelve hours, we had started to put high school days behind us and were now focusing on college.

My new challenging life was starting. That summer, I got comfortable with college life. I was away from home for the first time and taking on my own responsibilities. This was something that Coach Lambert wanted my roommate Ron Dixon and me to do. For the first time in our basketball careers, we were playing without our third guard, Oliver Purnell. So, we had to make that adjustment. He went to Old Dominion University in Virginia, but he visited us on occasion.

Summer classes covered a lot of material in a short period of time. They were difficult, but our first goal was to make it through the summer classes. If we did, our fall semester would be easier.

Only thirty-one students at Salisbury State College were African Americans. That count included full-time and part-time students. I felt right at home with that ratio, as it compared to the ratio at Stepen Decatur High School on my first day.

When it came to college, I had a lot to prove in the classroom. It didn't help when my high school English teacher told me I would never make it in college. *You aren't a very good student in this class. You won't do well in college.*

No matter how hard I tried, I couldn't please him. I was out to prove him wrong. He didn't have high expectations of me, but I believed in myself. The first class I took in college was English. I took English and World Civilization during the six-week summer session. I passed the courses, but the coach felt I could do better; that fall semester, I took the same classes over. I got my grades in the mail during winter break. I was so excited that I had received a B in English. What a Christmas gift!

I couldn't wait until my high school was back in session after the new year. When school opened, I walked down the hall to my old English teacher's class. I walked in his class, showed him my grade, then walked out without saying a word or even looking back. In my mind, I had shown him. By the time I got to my car I started to wonder. I wondered if he was sitting at his desk smiling and happy for me. I guess I will never know. I do know I had defied his expectations of me.

FALL BASEBALL SEASON

It was a learning process for me during my freshman year. I found out that every athlete was pretty good. Most looked in pretty good shape, too. When I first met Head Baseball Coach Deane Deshon, I was impressed with him right away. He seemed very confident and organized with his team practices. I did get the feeling that if you wanted to play for him, you had to earn it. When fall baseball season came around, I was prepared. I adjusted well to my new teammates. I was the fastest player on the team and of course the shortest. Playing baseball in the fall was a new experience for me. Traveling to play teams like the Naval Academy, Delaware State College, and Delaware Tech was fun. After a good fall season, I was ready for the spring season to begin. In speaking with Coach Deshon, I learned I was the first African American to play baseball for Salisbury State College.

MY BASKETBALL CAREER

I was thrilled to show my talents at the college level as I prepared for the upcoming basketball season. The walk across campus to the gymnasium seemed like a workout. All summer, Ron and I got a chance to work out in the college's Tawes Gymnasium. It was nice to get a jump on the other players before the season started. I was grateful to be in the gym because that was where our college games would be held. After going through a grueling pre-season of weightlifting—something I never did in high school—it was time for training. Coach Lambert didn't disappoint me. Many of the training sessions were team related. They were either timed or counted. During our suicide sprints, all team members had to complete the drill in a certain time. If not, the entire team would have to repeat the drill. If a certain number of free throws weren't made, the entire team had to run. I wasn't used to this. I always relied on what I did as an individual, but I couldn't on this team.

As the season was about to begin, an article in our local newspaper, the Daily Times, read,

> *Albin Handy is the shortest player on the squad at 5'4". Handy and Dixon were the backcourt men for Stephen Decatur last year. Handy is the fastest man on the squad and would become a vital cog in the Gulls defensive press.*

My dream had finally come true. I was playing on a college basketball team! I wanted that more than anything. I was the first athlete from Bishop, Maryland to play college basketball. I was excited for my family and my community more than anything; this was something for my family to be proud of. However, college basketball was a challenge for me. The level of competition was something I had never seen. All team players had all been the best players on their high school teams. They were bigger, stronger, and taller than any of the players in my high school days. However, the talent level on our Stephen Decatur team was strong.

Most high school athletes entering college want to play right away. I was no different. But I quickly realized that everyone was as good as me or better, so I needed to do something to separate myself...something that would make me stand out from my teammates. Again I relied on my speed, as I had always done.

What an outstanding opportunity to play college basketball. Some people didn't think I could make the high school team. Now I was competing at the college level. I enjoyed the trips to the different colleges. My favorite trip didn't even include playing in the game. Remember that Villanova Basketball Camp in high school? Well, during warmups at Lincoln University, the ball rolled out to half court. A Lincoln player picked the ball up, then handed it to me. When I looked up, it was my camp teammate. I never thought I would get to see him again. We exchanged handshakes and hugs. He was about 6'8". We became friends when we played on the championship team at camp. That night at Lincoln will be a night I will never forget.

I had a wonderful time playing on the team for a couple of years. The icing on the cake was that I was playing with Ron and another player from our state championship team, my cousin Milton Purnell. Milton arrived at Salisbury one year ahead of us. I had some good mentors in Duke Wright and Milton. They helped make my adjustment to college basketball easier. I also got to play with my good friend Wayne Briddell who had transferred in from Morgan State University. Wayne had played in my county for Worcester High School. Other teammates were Steve Gardner, Ken McLaughlin, Jack Stewart, Duke Wright, Lance Lewandowski, Mickey Calhoun, Gilbert Jenkins, Donald Hillock, and Sylvester Burke. Another player and one of my best friends was Richie Barber from Connecticut. He was a great ball handler who made spectacular passes.

I really enjoyed my time playing before I got injured. When one door closes, another one opens. I became a student assistant coach for Coach Lambert. During that time, we had a freshman team. I got to coach a few games by myself. One of my highlights was when I helped coach against the Czechoslovakia National Team in 1974. I also got to coach with my high school J.V. Coach Dick Burbage, who was on the staff. Not bad for the kid from the small town of Bishop.

MY SPRING BASEBALL CAREER

Coming off an outstanding high school baseball career, I thought I was going to be a star right away. When spring baseball rolled around my freshman year, I was so excited. The thought of playing for head coach Deane Deshon seemed like a dream come true. I had put out 110% during our workouts…doing well enough to be a starter when the season began, I thought. However, I was so disappointed when I didn't make the starting lineup. There were starters from the previous year who were returning. The fact that I was an incoming freshman didn't make it easy for my coach. I had to keep working and wait for my opportunity. Every athlete at the college level had incredible skills. I had to adjust to that fact. Don't get me wrong—I wanted to be on the field. It was hard to take at first.

I played a little here and there, pinch-running for the most part, giv-ing me the opportunity to steal some bases. I kept practicing hard and giv-ing 100% during wind sprints. I think it was about the fourth or fifth game when I got the call. I was sitting on the bench talking to another freshman player before the game. Coach Deshon called the starting lineup and some-one said I was in it for the first time in my career.

One of the other freshmen said, *Hondo, you're starting!*

I looked for my glove, grabbed it, and I was so nervous at that very moment that I stumbled out of the dugout. I had waited all season for my name to be called. I raced to the outfield. Standing in the outfield, all I could think of was giving it my all that day. *Is this the day that I become a starter for the rest of the season?* I never wanted to come out of the starting lineup again. However, I found myself rotating in and out of the lineup. I had a fantastic first season, leading the team in stolen bases for most of the season. I learned to hit from both sides of the plate. Coach wanted me to bat left-handed against right-handed pitchers. He said, *I want you to be a little closer to first base when you bat. This will allow you to take advantage of your speed, especially on your drag bunts.* He then introduced us to this big thick-handled bamboo bat. I was able to use it sometimes, but it was hard to get used to.

I really enjoyed our southern trips in the spring. It was still cold in March up North when we started our season. The whistling wind would blow our baseball caps across the field. I felt a stinging pain each time I made contact with the ball during batting practice. It was so cold—at times just playing catch hurt. My fingers tended to get numb from the chilly air, leaving the tips of my fingers with no feeling. It was a challenge to grip the ball. Dressing warm helped, but it was still easy to get that early spring cold. Sniffing the entire practice was a norm for all players.

It was exciting to compete against some of the schools in the South. The weather was much warmer down South. We competed against teams such as Campbell College, Fayetteville State University, Newberry College, The Citadel, University of North Carolina at Wilmington, and Francis Marion College.

One thing that I was sad to see down South: at times I saw signs that still said *Whites Only*. I didn't let that bother me too much, although that season I was the only African American on the team. I had great teammates, so I wasn't too worried. I do remember the players decided we were going out one night since we didn't have a game against the Citadel until the next day. We were enjoying ourselves when a bunch of guys on the other side of the building started singing *Dixie*. I was immediately ready to go.

But my teammates said, *Don't worry about them, Hondo.*

I was okay for a while, until my baseball teammates started singing *Yankee Doddle*. The louder they got, the louder my teammates got. I started to get a little nervous…let's face it—a lot nervous. I was so upset that I found the only phone in the place.

I called my Aunt HaHa and said, *I love you. My college baseball team is down South playing. We are at this establishment, and I don't know if I am going to make it out of this place. If I don't, just know that I put up a good fight. I love you. Tell my mother I love her too.*

My teammates were ready to fight if we had to, but luck was on my side. I got my team out of there as fast as I could. I kept reminding them that we were supposed to be on our way back to our rooms very soon.

My teammates were always putting me in awkward situations. One evening when we were at the University of North Carolina at Wilmington, we were housed in a military-type facility. Of course, I took the bunk all the way in the back. I did this so I could keep an eye on my teammates, as they liked to play pranks and joke about things.

I was about to call it a night when one of the players shouted, *Hondo there is someone here to see you!*
I said, *You guys aren't going to fool me this time.*
Then more teammates started shouting, *There really is someone here to see you.*

I still didn't believe them.

Next Coach Deshon said, *Hondo, you have a visitor.*
I said, *Coach, are you in on this too?*
He said, *No, but we don't want to let him in until you identify him.*

I slowly got up and took the long walk to the front of the room. I could see my teammates laughing. I just kept thinking, *Oh no…what are these guys up to?* When I got to the front door, Coach opened it. In an instant, I jumped into the arms of one of my former classmates from high school, Frank Benvenuto. What a relief. I just knew they were trying to pull another fast one on me.

Frank was attending the University of North Carolina at Wilmington. He knew our team was playing at his school. He just wanted to see me. Frank and I still joke about that experience. There are other stories to tell, but I'll move on with my baseball career.

The next two seasons saw me starting to hit for extra bases. I could feel myself getting better. I also got to play with my new friends, Jerry West from Philadelphia and Milton Williams from Baltimore. I still get teased at home about a headline from our local newspapers which stated, *Little Albin Comes In Handy. Florence, South Carolina-Little 5' 5" Albin Handy socked a tie-breaking single in the fifth inning to give Salisbury State a 3-2 victory over Francis Marion College.*

After my junior season, Assistant Coach Mike McGlinchey suggested that I keep playing throughout the summer. *I am going to get you in a summer league,* he said. *I think the competition will help you improve.* He got me on a team in Wilmington, Delaware. I lived with my brother Ronald and his wife Peggy in Philadelphia. I traveled to Wilmington by train for each game. It was perfect because my sister Dianna lived in Wilmington. She was able to meet me at the train station then take me to the games. After the game, she would take me to the train station to return to Philly. I had a great summer playing baseball. I was playing with some of the top college players on the East Coast and some former professional players. This only increased my love for the game of baseball.

Unfortunately, the very first day back to college for my senior year, I broke my patella. This meant I was probably done with sports for the entire year. As we drove onto campus to unload my luggage, I had my family back the car up by the window of my first-floor room. My roommate and I always left a sliding window open in our room for easy access.

I said, *Just drop my stuff inside the window; I am going to go play basketball.*

I could see some of my teammates playing outdoor basketball when we drove up. I couldn't wait to get out there. I ran down the hallway of my dorm, Choptank Hall. I dashed out the back door to the court. I could see my family waving as they were leaving.

Not long after I arrived, someone let me in the game. I went down the court once. The second time down the court, as I was going in for a layup, someone undercut me. I landed with my right knee bent. My knee hit the asphalt first, breaking my patella. I experienced excruciating pain.

I could hear my roommate Ron say, *Get up, Hondo, get up...*something he always said when one of us fell. But I couldn't get up this time. I said, *I don't think I have a knee anymore.*

Someone then called an ambulance. Luckily, the hospital was just down the street. Back then we didn't have cell phones, so my mother and aunt had to wait until they got home to find out what had happened. I was probably in the hospital before they got out of Salisbury. The doctors prepared for an immediate operation of wiring my patella (kneecap) back together.

The surgery was successful. The fluid in my knee caused the area to swell to an enormous size. My first cast was twice the size of my knee. I was in so much pain. I was in more pain after the operation than before. I remember thinking that if I ever had kids, I would not allow them to play sports. I would never want them to go through the pain that I was suffering. I didn't want my mother to know how much pain I was in. She might want me to come home.

In the middle of the night, six of my roommates came into my room to see me. Feeling drowsy from all the medicine, I thought it was the nurse coming back in. When I saw them I said, *Visiting hours are over; how did you get in?* But that didn't stop them. They were so noisy. I think they had been partying. I was so glad when they left because I was hurting.

After I was released from the hospital, I was in two different casts for about twelve weeks. On crutches, I still attended all my classes. My roommates in my cluster helped me for the entire semester. I was so thankful for that.

I had one of the best trainers in the country in Hunter Smith. After having my second cast removed; my leg was entirely straight. He put me through some of the most grueling rehabilitation that I had ever experienced. Rehab was twice a day—early in the morning before class and again after class. He would drag me out of bed and send me to the training room if I overslept. He didn't let me off the hook, even when my knee was giving me a lot of pain.

He said, *We've got to get your knee bending again*. It was so straight; I didn't think it was possible to bend it again. My first exercise was to let my leg hang off the edge of the table. This allowed the weight of the leg to help bend my knee. I yelled so loud from the pain. When I looked, my leg had not bent at all. Next, I would lay on my stomach, with a weighted attachment on my foot. Hunter would use a crank to help bend my knee. It inflicted so much pain that I would shout to stop, please stop. The first time he did it, I thought my knee had bent a good deal.

When I asked him, he said, *It bent about an inch. We have a long way to go. You are babying your knee.* So he asked my roommate, Ron, to take me out to the track. Hunter wanted him to make me run with him.

Ron held me up so I wouldn't fall. Although I almost fell with every step, we made it around the track the first time. He kept making me try to run around the track. Then it was weight training with my knee. It was a long process. I owe a lot to Hunter and Ron. They got me walking and running again. Hunter even used my knee as an example in his training class—the students had a chance to look at my knee!

Hunter had been an assistant athletic trainer for the Miami Dolphins before coming to Salisbury. He went on to become the head trainer for the Baltimore Colts and then the Indianapolis Colts for the next twenty-three years, so I was in good hands.

Before I left Salisbury, I became an assistant coach for the baseball team with my good friend Dr. Tom Stitcher, under Coach Deshon. What an honor. To top it off, I got to play with and coach my old high school teammate Ron Rickards. Who would have ever thought that I would be coaching baseball in college?

MY SOCCER CAREER

Everyone loved our soccer coach, Coach Ben Maggs. You could always tell it was him coming by the way he walked—always on his toes. Coach Maggs was very popular and a legend on campus. I got a chance to play for Coach Maggs and loved every minute of it. He had been around campus so long that they eventually named the new athletic facility in his honor. He was a funny guy known for his strange walk.

In our area, Pocomoke High School produced the best soccer players. They were Maryland State Champions year after year. Things didn't seem to change when I got to college. I played against my teammates David Byrd, Allan Byrd, and Tom Wescott from Pocomoke when we were in high school. Then there was an All-American Soccer Player, Bobby Thomas from Pocomoke. Players from Pocomoke kept coming to Salisbury. Each year our team got better and better.

I remember when we played Lincoln University and I think ten of eleven of Salisbury's starters were from Pocomoke. I did get in to score my first goal of the season against Lincoln. My score came on an assist from Harry Winters. The team on our schedule that I couldn't wait to play against was Old Dominion University. My high school teammate Oliver Purnell attended ODU. It was a special trip for me because I got a chance to see my old teammate. However, that was the highlight of my day, as our team did not play very well. I did enjoy playing on the first Astro Turf field. Playing soccer at Salisbury was another dream come true. As I look back, I can't believe I played so many sports in college.

INDOOR TRACK & FIELD

Track & Field was always a favorite of mine in high school. I thought I was a very good sprinter, plus I loved competing in the long jump. I found out Jeff Polk, a local track star, was a member of the Salisbury State track team. I decided I wanted to be on the team, too. He was a Maryland high school state champion. We became very good friends, on and off the track. I was the fastest on the baseball, basketball, and soccer teams. I wanted to see how I matched up against the best in the school and one of the best in the country.

In between fall baseball and basketball, I got a chance to run indoor track for Coach Lloyd Sigler. Most of our training took place inside, down the halls of one of our classroom buildings. We were unable to use starting blocks in the halls, but we did the best we could. Coach Sigler made us do distance running, even those of us who were sprinters. Racing all over town wasn't fun, but it was part of our training.

There were no indoor track facilities on campus. Using halls for Indoor Track & Field might have seemed strange in the '70s, but it was good enough for us. Today, high school track teams train in the hallways of their schools all the time. Sprinting up and down the halls led to us sweating the entire time. Trying to come out of the starting blocks was going to be vital for me. During winter break, I practiced over and over at home trying to master the starting blocks.

I was quick to find out that I was no longer the fastest person on this team. That title belonged to my teammate, the great Jeff Polk. Jeff ended up being a four-time All-American MVP in track. He holds six school records and was also selected to the All-Decade track team of the '70s.

The speedster Polk and I got a chance to run in several notable meets including the Philadelphia Track Classic and the Atlantic AAU Indoor Championships. What an experience! At Essex Community College in Baltimore, I ran 5.8 seconds in the 50 meters. Jeff finished first in the field at 5.4 seconds. The world record for the 50 meters was 5.2 seconds. I suffered a leg injury at the South Atlantic AAU Indoor at the Catonsville Community College Championship. I pulled so many leg muscles running track, I guess because I was trying so hard.

STUDENT ASSISTANT INTRAMURAL DIRECTOR

My opportunities just kept coming in college. Being involved in sports was very important to me. Because I was still recovering from my broken patella in my senior year, I couldn't participate on any of my college teams. Instead, I got a chance to become a student assistant intramural director under Director Grady Armstrong. Through this position, I was able to learn the ins and outs of the different intramural programs. I learned all the rules and regulations of the sports leagues. I engaged and worked with the student game officials. I was a physical education major, but this was a learning experience for me. This opportunity proved to be something positive for me during my recovery. I later took advantage of the experience and listed it on my resume.

SALUTE TO COACH WARD LAMBERT

Young people are often unable to find a mentor. I was lucky to have someone outside of my family whom I looked up to. For me, that person was my basketball coach, Ward Lambert. I will always be thankful to him for being there for me. He taught me so much in high school and our relationship continued in college. He was not only my best coach and a great teacher; over time he became a father figure for me. I know he was hard on me, but it was for the right reasons. Nothing came easy with him—including those practices. He was even harder in kinesiology class. He never gave me anything. He made me earn it. I respected him then, and I respect him now.

I am so glad I had the opportunity to share the basketball court with him. It all paid off when we won the Maryland State Basketball Championship. That was the highlight of my high school career. I am thankful to have had him as my coach. I am also thankful for him allowing me to be a part of the Salisbury State College basketball team, then later allowing me to be an assistant coach for the team.

I took advantage of our relationship. I asked Coach Lambert to be the first basketball camp director at the Ocean City Recreation & Parks Department. He told me he'd be happy to, and he even returned during the winter to provide free clinics for our department. I am so grateful for everything he did for me. Although in high school, when I approached him about my brand-new game warm-up suit being too big, Coach Lambert said, *Hondo, they were made for basketball players.* That was so embarrassing; I am still shaking my head as I recall that one.

Then there was the time he officiated for our pickup basketball game—the game between members of my Salisbury State players and Talvin Skinner's University of Maryland Eastern Shore players. When Talvin, my 6'6" friend who went on to star for the NBA's Seattle Supersonics, dribbled over my head, I was sure it was a violation. However, Coach didn't call it.

Talk about an embarrassing moment… He said, *His hand was on the top of the ball, so it is not a violation.*

Coach Lambert has been a great mentor to me. I have always respected his opinion. I always call him before I make a major decision in my life. He has made me a better person.

CHAPTER 21

MY GREATEST ACADEMIC ACHIEVEMENT—AND I'M ON STRIKE

Everybody has an event they will always remember. What I will always look back on is an academic achievement. That day came when my grandmother got to see me receive my college degree. I was the first family member to earn a degree from a four-year institution. I wondered what was going through her mind. I could tell she was thrilled, as were my Aunt Middy and Aunt Ionia. When I was growing up, this seemed like an unattainable accomplishment—unbelievable, really—but not for my mother. She really believed that I could compete academically on any level. She believed that I could defy expectations in the classroom. I was so excited that I finally completed college credits required for me to graduate. I graduated in December; this meant the school systems nearby were in the middle of their academic year. I started applying for teaching positions in Wicomico and Worcester Counties. When I graduated on that Friday afternoon, I had the weekend to celebrate.

Throughout the final couple of semesters, I had a part-time job at UPS. I worked from the early morning until 10:00 a.m. On the Monday morning following graduation, I headed to work. Still in shape, I raced down College Avenue through the UPS gates on Lake Street. When I reached the gate, I noticed a stranger standing there.

When I tried to pass him, he said, *Where are you going?*

I am headed to work.

You work here?

Yes, and you're making me late.

He then said, *We are on strike; pick up one of those signs and walk in the picket line.*

I couldn't believe it. I had just graduated. On my first working day since graduating, I was on strike. I didn't even know what we were on strike for. There were a lot of guys on the picket line I had never seen before. Later, I learned that they were from the Teamsters Union in Baltimore. When I found out we would still be getting a check at the end of the week, I didn't care. Each day I came to work and marched up and down the sidewalk. On Friday, we were instructed to go to South Salisbury Boulevard to pick up our checks. This was where the Union office was located. There was already a line of UPS workers waiting. When I reached the window and told them my name, they gave me an envelope. I started walking away, then I decided to open my envelope. To my surprise, the check was for $25. I had walked all week for $25! Well—that was the last straw for me. I had to make an immediate decision about my future.

CHAPTER 22

HARFORD COUNTY, MARYLAND AND THE RETURN HOME

I took that $25, filled my gas tank, loaded my car with everything I could, and said goodbye to my room on College Avenue. I was so excited about starting my new adventure, but at the same time a little sad about leaving the Eastern Shore of Maryland—a place I had called home all my life. But I had no choice; it was time to begin my next challenge. I used a map that I had picked up at a gas station and headed across the Chesapeake Bay Bridge. I was nervous because I had never driven in so much traffic. Cars everywhere were speeding past me like I was standing still. I was quick to learn that the speed limit was for the slow traffic lane. Horns blowing, drivers cutting in and out of lanes...I felt like it was the Indy 500 or the Dover Downs Monster Mile. I was so relieved when I reached my friend Lonnie Mercer's house.

Lonnie had been my next door neighbor and high school basketball teammate. He entered the Marine Corps after high school while I went to college. I was so proud of him to have the courage to join the Marines. He even did a six-week training during the summer after his junior year. I still have some of the letters he mailed me from basic training in Camp Lejeune, North Carolina and in Okinawa, Japan. After leaving the Marines, he found employment in the United States Post Office in Baltimore and an evening job at Johns Hopkins Hospital.

Lonnie invited me to come live with him. To top it off, he had a job for me. I couldn't turn it down. The day after I arrived, I was employed at Johns Hopkins Hospital as a security guard. The shift from midnight to 8:00 am was perfect. I had to get used to that schedule, but it worked out just fine. I put in teaching applications for the next school year and for substitute teaching positions. It was now January and I just hoped to get my foot in the door. I would speed down Pulaski Highway from Baltimore to Edgewood to check the answering machine. I would check to see if any school needed me to substitute that day. When I was tired, I always seemed to get a call from a school in need. When I felt good, no school needed a substitute.

I never realized how lucky I was to grow up on the Eastern Shore of Maryland, until I worked in Baltimore. Working security at Johns Hopkins Hospital was a story within itself. We wore uniforms that looked just like the Baltimore City Police uniforms. I was told this was to make it look like there were police officers everywhere. Anyway, the first week we got paid, I asked my co-workers what they were doing for the weekend.

To my surprise they said, We're going to Ocean City.

Why Ocean City?
Because we must get away from Baltimore and relax at the beach.

Lonnie thought I should drive around the streets of Baltimore to familiarize myself with the city. As I drove around, I begin to realize how much I appreciated where I had lived my entire life. We had lots of space, beautiful parks, recreation, the beach, attractions, amusements, the board-walk, the small-town atmosphere, Fisher's Popcorn, Thrasher's French Fries, and the Atlantic Ocean. What was I doing in Baltimore?

In between the substitute teaching and security, Lonnie kept me busy. He would say, *Let's go play some ball; we have a couple hours before work.* Because of his military status, we played most of the time at Edgewood Arsenal Army Base. On the weekends, members of our state championship basketball team would come up to play. We felt like we were back in high school on the court.

After a while, I got a long-term substitute job at Edgewood Elementary School. One day before class, I noticed a note on the bulletin board. The note indicated that Harford County Parks & Recreation was looking for an after-school youth basketball director at Edgewood Elementary. I knew I could do that. Basketball was something that I loved; teaching kids the game was something I enjoyed; plus, the kids would be from Edgewood Elementary. I would get to meet more parents from the community. This could help me get my foot in the door for the next school year. Excited, I contacted the parks & recreation director, Paul Yanney. I was so delighted that I got the position. It was a wonderful experience. The Harford County Youth Basketball League job led to me being employed at the school's summer camp.

After a while, things stopped going well for me. I started hanging out with the wrong crowd. The teaching position I was seeking never came. I had a serious conversation with my brother, Ronald. With his encouragement, I decided to come home. He told me to go home and start my life over—so that's what I did.

CHAPTER 23

THE BERLIN MUNICIPAL YOUTH BASKETBALL LEAGUE

I returned home with the itch for recreation. I started a small recreation program for the kids in Berlin. A small grant allowed me to provide all kinds of board games, indoor volleyball, and karate. I even took a group of boys to Skateland in Salisbury. When no help came to transport the boys that day, I loaded as many as I could in my car and took them to Skateland. I then returned to Berlin to pick up the rest and take them to Salisbury. I did the same to get them home. I did the same with a group of basketball players for our all-star game in Salisbury, making two round trips to Salisbury's Lake Street Basketball Courts.

Next Gregory Purnell and I decided to start the community's first summer boys' basketball program. We put together a game plan. We decided the name of the program would be the Berlin Municipal Youth Basketball League. Games were played outdoors at the William Henry Park in Berlin. After the first two years, the games were moved indoors to Berlin Middle School.

The kids had a fantastic time. The parents loved it because their children had something to look forward to. We painted the lines at our local basketball courts, added a three-point line, put up new nets, and got some player benches. Councilman Sonny Adkins fixed the basketball rims. He also opened the league by tossing up the first jump ball. We reached out to area businesses and organizations for team sponsorships. We were able to purchase league shirts for each team, scoreboards, and clocks. We even had the games filmed! With the help of Frank Snyder, Town Administrator, the Town of Berlin offered to pay for our league insurance. We had donations from Sam Henry and Dennis Brown. Rick Cullen of the Daily Times covered our game results. Great appreciation goes out to the coaches, Jim Beard, Donald Tunnell, Sam White, Gary Smith, Gary Oliver, Pat Henry, Mark Bowen, Drake Bowen, Calvin Jarmon, Reggie Truitt, Greg Hall, Quinten (Bo Peep) Dennis, Brazil Briddell, Larry Duffy, Richard Mumford, Robert Mumford, and Fulton Holland.

Post-season games were against the Snow Hill All-Stars and the Salisbury All-Stars. At the end of each season, we reserved the pavilion at Stephen Decatur Park for our picnic and awards ceremony. Coach Ward Lambert, Head Coach of Salisbury State College, was our guest speaker. He also handed out the awards. We offered the program for five years.

I think that league helped many kids. There are many success stories. I will mention two: Andre Foreman and Shawn Harris.

Andre was a very good basketball player in our youth league. He constantly showed good sportsmanship; his demeanor never changed on the court. Whether the official made a bad call or good call, he never seemed to question the outcome. I am so proud of him having the ability to control his emotions throughout his playing days. Andre Foreman went on to play basketball for Stephen Decatur High School.

Following high school, he became a standout player for Salisbury State College, finishing with 17 school records. He became a Two-Time All-American player. He became the all-time collegiate leading scorer in Division III history. He later enjoyed an eighteen-year professional basketball career overseas. The entire town of Berlin was so excited when he was inducted into The Salisbury Athletics Hall of Fame in 2002. He surpassed that by being enshrined into the Small College Basketball National Hall of Fame Class of 2020.

Shawn Harris was always interested in becoming a better person and basketball player. We had life conversations every Saturday morning as we left to get our Egg McMuffins at McDonald's. After we arrived home, he would take the shortcut to the basketball courts by jumping this big ditch not far from his grandmother's house. He continued to improve during his play in our league. He went on to have a great career playing for Stephen Decatur High School.

Following high school, Shawn enrolled in the United States Marine Corp. The decorated military veteran of eight years settled in California. He established the Triangle and Two Foundation, a leadership academy whose mission is to provide resources to stimulate education, leadership, and social growth through sports development. He is currently dean of athletics at Westcliff University, assistant principal at Westcliff Preparatory Academy, and a WNBA agent.

Not bad for two young kids who started their sports careers in the Berlin Municipal Youth Basketball League. The things they learned in our youth league regarding good sportsmanship and character building seemed to stick with them throughout their successful careers. Andre and Shawn represent the small areas of Flower Street, Germantown, and Ironshire—where everyone from 21811 resides and cheers them on.

CHAPTER 24

WELCOME BACK TO OCEAN CITY, MARYLAND

Have you ever felt that you couldn't wait to graduate just to move away from home? Well, that was how I felt. Sometimes things don't go as planned—so welcome back to the place I hoped to get away from.

After a few months of looking for employment, I learned of a position that came open in Ocean City. Gregory Purnell encouraged me to apply for that job. He said, *I think this would be perfect for you.* The program gave me the opportunity to work mainly in the Parks Division of the Ocean City Recreation & Parks Department. It also allowed me to work with some after school programs. I was officially hired full-time by Gerald Groves, Director of Recreation & Parks at the time. I will always be grateful to him. I started working on January 3, 1980. Although things did not go well for me at first, Gerry—or Cheese, as we called him— stuck with me.

He said, *Hondo I believed in you because you have so much to offer.* He continued to encourage me almost every day. When I started, the department's office was located on 3rd Street. I have always told people we operated out of the back door of City Hall…in a gymnasium that was located inside the building that used to be a school. I have seen so many changes in the department throughout the years. I have witnessed many events and stories in the making, some that I plan to share in this book.

CHAPTER 25

A LITTLE OCEAN CITY
RECREATION & PARKS HISTORY

Recreation & Parks in Ocean City didn't just happen—there is a history. I want to share some of the most interesting stories and events that happened during my career. For the recreation professionals across the country, I hope that reading my stories will encourage you to put your stories in writing. I am sure those who follow you will be inspired by your stories. But before the stories, I want to share a little history about Ocean City Recreation & Parks. I had to do some research, so I am relying on the memories of others for a lot of the information. I also highlighted a few things about the directors I worked with during my career.

JD QUILLIN AND NORMAN CATHELL

According to JD Quillin and Norman Cathell of the Ocean City Lions Club, youth activities got starting in the early 1960s. Cathell was working for the police department. In 1961, he was encouraged by Chief of Police Jack Phillips to start a Police Boys and Girls Club. The police department was located on Dorchester Street. The club met once a week on the second floor of the building behind the department that was used for indoor sports games. That all changed with the storm of 1962; it became necessary to dissolve the program due to inadequate facilities. On 3rd Street, where City Hall is today, there was a school, there was a gym, and the 3rd Street Ball Field. But after the storm, under the direction of the National Guard, trash and wood were brought to 3rd Street to burn. Of course, the wood was eventually completely burned, and the field was able to be used again.

Around late 1962 or early 1963, it was suggested that organizations plan programs for children and youths. That ended up with Cathell and Quillin starting the recreation council, as they saw a real need for the children in the community to have something to do after school, over the weekends, and during the summer months. They got some volunteers to help, as most activities were outside games. Norman and JD both coached. Baseball and soccer were outdoors while basketball and volleyball were held indoors in the gym along with other activities. There was also an adult softball group. JD said, *We would come down and play volleyball during lunch.*

DIRECTOR OLLIE BRADFORD

The Lions Club hired Ollie Bradford to be the first director, as Cathell and Quillin of the Lions Club were busy starting the council. Things started off well. They worked with the Little League organization and even had a dance at City Hall. But after three years, the Lions Club was moving in a new direction. Meanwhile, JD and Paul Bodolus built the football field on 4th Street, next to the bay. It was an empty field, so they just began working on it. They started building and when the bills started coming in, they would go door to door to raise money to pay the bills. George Gumm, a Lions Club member, worked for the Ocean City Golf Club as the greenskeeper. He helped by irrigating the baseball field on 3rd Street.

DIRECTOR TOM BROWN

As Norman and JD were interviewing various people to be the new director, Tom Brown came to see them about the job. Tom played for the Green Bay Packers for four years under Vince Lombardi and had four championship rings. After football, he played two years for the Washington Senators baseball team. Tom immediately got efforts more organized.

Football got started and he planned more activities. Citizens saw the results of what Tom and the Lions Club were doing. With the involvement of many children and more programs, this organization was transformed into a city department.

DIRECTOR GARY ARTHUR

After graduating from Clemson University on a football scholarship in 1972, Gary Arthur was hired in Ocean City. He was the director of Ocean City Recreation & Parks for six years and added thirty-nine new recreational programs for the city residents during his tenure. I heard some good stories about Gary, not only about how great of a job he did, but some exciting stories about the Ocean City Men's Football League. I never got to work for Gary; however, my co-workers Greg and Ron Rickards did. I did get the opportunity to network with him in the Maryland Recreation & Parks Association. He shared many stories about his time in Ocean City.

DIRECTOR GERALD GROVES

Gerald Groves served as the director from 1978 to 1984. I was hired by Gerald (Cheese) Groves and under his guidance, I got my career started. When things weren't going well for me, he continued to encourage me. I met with him several times in his office. Each time, he kept telling me that I had so much to offer and not to give up. I really wanted to work with kids. I was a scorekeeper for our softball leagues under Mr. Groves. I also coached Little League baseball under his direction. I believe that because of Director Groves, we have Northside Park today. He got things started with a vision of Northside. I also believe Cheese improved the Parks division under the leadership of Calvin Ginnavan. The Sunfest Softball Tournament expanded during Gerald's tenure.

DIRECTOR TOM PERLOZZO

Tom Perlozzo was the director from 1985 to 1998. He brought lots of changes to Ocean City and expanded our department. He oversaw the growth and development of the fifty-eight acres of the Northside Park Complex, the municipally owned Eagle's Landing Golf Course, Ocean City beach patrol, the Winterfest of Lights, and other special events.

When Perlozzo became director, he met with each of his employees. He asked me where I wanted to be in the next five years. Without hesitation I told him *I want to be a programmer. I think I can do the job.* Maybe a year later, I got the opportunity to become a recreation specialist. I thank Tom every day for believing in me. He was a hands-on director. He was also a participant in most of our adult programs. That meant he was always around and could see firsthand how the programs were being run. He taught me a lot.

DIRECTOR TOM SHUSTER

In 1998, Tom Shuster became the director and held that position for nearly sixteen years. Under his direction, the arena, the development of Sunset Park, and a dog playground at Little Salisbury became additions to our recreation and parks system. Other additions included Fiesta Park Pavilion, the softball pavilion, the footbridge, Military Flag Plaza, a grant-funded replacement of playgrounds, and an installation of an outdoor exercise and fitness area. Sometimes his delegation style seemed a bit different from what we were used to; however, his leadership was effective. Under Tom, my title was changed to Recreation Supervisor.

DIRECTOR SUSAN PETITO

Susan Petito started with the department in 1986. She became the director in 2014, and began the director's position overseeing the development of four division budgets: program, parks, administration, and golf course. I was so glad that Susan got the opportunity to be the director. She served as assistant director for many years. Susan and I worked together on a few programs when I first started with the program division. Many nights, Susan and I were the last to leave the building. Susan was a pleasure to work with. I am sure many of her employees feel the same. Susan has been with the department for nearly 36 years. She knows the ins and outs of the department, having served under Perlozzo and Shuster. The department is in good hands with Ms. Petito, as I called her.

CHAPTER 26

STARTING MY NEW ROLE IN OCEAN CITY

As I grew up, I don't think anyone in Bishop expected that I would ever be employed at Ocean City's City Hall. After all, not that long before I started, African Americans were only cleaning hotels or working in restaurant kitchens. I was so nervous, but thrilled at the same time. Before I got this job, I had been inside City Hall to play basketball—and only to play basketball. So, this was a kind of homecoming for me.

Our duties included maintaining the basketball courts inside City Hall, 3rd and 4th Street Ball Fields, the Skate Park, the outdoor basketball courts on 4th Street, tennis, and basketball courts at 41st Street, and the Tennis Center at 61st Street.

Our supervisor at the time was Barry Fisher. My crew included Greg Purnell and Ron Rickards. Kevin Hudson later joined our team. Barry would explain what we would be doing each day. Then off we would go in our old Army truck to do our duties. (Our department also owned an old blue school bus.)

Our assistant director at the time was Eric Mickolasko. He mainly organized programs which we would assist with after school. I got a small taste of promoting programs when Eric was about to cancel our youth basketball league. He said, *We don't have enough kids registered to have a league. So, I am going to cancel the program.*

My co-workers, Greg, Ron, Kevin, and I convinced Eric to allow us to go over to Ocean City Elementary School. That was where most of our participants went to school. We had this portable basketball basket goal that we transported over to the school. We must have gotten the principal to allow the students to come down to the cafeteria. We set up the basket and brought some basketballs. We put together this inspirational clinic for the kids as if we were the Ocean City Globetrotters. The students enjoyed our demonstration so much that registration quickly filled. The Ocean City youth basketball program was saved! I will never forget how we did that. I will be forever grateful to Greg, Ronnie, and Kevin, as I didn't want the league to be canceled. I was so inspired to see what a little thinking outside the box could lead to.

Other programs that were going on in the mid-80s were Little League Baseball; Little League Softball; men's softball; women's softball; indoor volleyball; indoor skating; and adult men's and women's basketball. Youth football had just ended. We had a very good men's league that played on 3rd and 4th Streets. Later we constructed an adult softball field at Ocean City Elementary School. We also had a Little League field at the school. Our women's softball league attracted lots of spectators each week. We were very successful with both adult leagues. We probably had twenty or so teams in our men's Tuesday/Thursday League and our Sunday League. There were about twelve teams in the women's league. The league was so popular that almost every restaurant or bar downtown sponsored a team.

Keeping score for the men's softball league was an honor for me. This allowed me to meet everyone in the league. I met hundreds of softball players; some were business owners, bar owners, restaurant owners, police officers, and lawyers. This position lasted a few years. I interacted with so many people, many of whom I went to college with, including Steve Pappas and Tom Dickerson, owners of the Original Greene Turtle.

Not long after that, Calvin Ginnavan became the park superintendent. We were on our way to becoming a bonified Parks division. The

"4Ever Four"—Calvin, Ron, Greg, and me—was formed. Cal expanded our department from not only maintaining ball fields, but any city-owned property in Ocean City. Because of our perfectionism, the maintenance and care of outside properties at City Hall, Entrance Park, and other areas became our responsibilities. Public Works was responsible for this in the past.

Soon after Mr. Ginnavan became park superintendent, I became the first public grounds specialist for Ocean City. Calvin, Councilwomen Louis Gulyas, and I reinvigorated the beautification committee for the Town of Ocean City. Under the leadership of Director Groves, the concept of Northside Park began at City Hall and became a reality with the groundbreaking on 125th Street. While Northside was getting started, the Parks division begin to expand. It relocated to 41st Street and then 65th Street before reaching Northside Park. We began to beautify the city, planting trees from Downtown Baltimore Avenue to 30th Street. Later we planted trees at 94th Street and maintained all city-owned bulkhead areas. We made mini-parks in these small areas, laying sod and planting flowers. Meanwhile, we still had to take care of all the ball fields. The "4Ever Four"—Greg, Ron, Calvin, and I—were extremely dedicated, as we all stayed employed by the Recreation & Parks Department for over 35 years.

CHAPTER 27
LOSING BY 100 POINTS

Since we were able to get enough players for the youth basketball league, I was excited to get the league started. I became a referee. I played high school and college basketball, so I was used to making calls—the correct way. I was calling walking, double dribbling, up and down—all the traditional infractions. Many players didn't like the calls I was making.

One player asked, *What are you calling?!*
Traveling…you took two steps without dribbling.
His response? *We usually get three steps.*

Since we had a very small gymnasium, some of the rules had to be altered—something I didn't know. The out-of-bounds line was about 6" from the wall, all the way around the gym. When the ball was taken out of bounds, the players were standing on the out-of-bounds line. We had to tell the opposing team players to let the players throw the ball in. If a player got a rebound, I was instructed to tell the other team to fall back. This allowed players to dribble to half-court, where the defense could guard them again. So many changes to normal basketball play…At the end of the season, our assistant director Eric asked:

Would you like to be the All-Star coach? You would coach the 10 – 12-Year-Old Division at the Salvation Army Basketball Tournament.
I said, *No way; those kids don't even like me because of the calls I was making.*

Well, the coaches think you know a lot about basketball. They were just parents trying to help.

I thought about it for a few minutes. I begin to feel a sense of pride. I agreed to coach the team, since I was competitive about team play and the teams I worked with. I did some things that are probably not allowed today in recreation. I held two weeks of closed practices; no parents were allowed. I even locked the City Hall gym doors, so as not to be interrupted. Again... something that wouldn't be allowed today.

I had to train the players on how to play against a defensive press to prepare for tournament play. At the tournament, if a player got a rebound, the opposing players would try to take the ball away. They would not be falling back to mid-court, so my players had to adjust to this. My next priority was to teach the team to properly press their opponents. After a couple of weeks drilling these new rules into their heads, I saw progress. It was time for the players to receive their uniforms; they were very excited.

The afternoon of the tournament, the kids filled up the old Army bus Eric told me to drive to the Salvation Army. Talk about some smiling faces and enthusiastic children! They were so happy to be traveling together. I really did feel the kids were prepared to play. Ocean City had never won a game in this tournament. Could this be the night? I remember it just like it was today. Eric had told me, *Hondo drive the kids over to the game and after the game, drive straight back...no stopping.*

Upon arriving in Salisbury, I gave the team a quick talk and we unloaded everything off the bus. When the kids walked inside of the Salvation Army facility, I knew the game was over. They lost their focus. They kept saying, *Wow! This place is so big...look at the baskets. They are so high! This court is longer than ours. Where did all those people come from?* They were just standing there looking around in awe, not moving at all.

In their defense, they were comparing the Salvation Army Gymnasium to our gym. I finally got them to the bench to begin warming up. When they saw the Salisbury team, they started to question the players' ages. To be honest, they did look big. I tried to explain that we only had four teams to choose our All-Star players from and they had around a dozen teams. They simply had a larger pool of players to draw upon. We were limited in our total number of players and had to choose three players, regardless of their size, from each of our four teams. My guys didn't understand that.

The game was about to start, so I gave them last-minute instructions. We were having trouble getting the ball up the court. Salisbury, our opponent, was the best team in the tournament. As expected, they were very aggressive. The tournament rules allowed me four time-outs for the game. I should have used one time out during each quarter. However, I used up all my time-outs for the game in the first quarter. My players were so tired. We were already losing so badly. I had to come up with a strategy that would help my team. I asked them to foul the other players when I told them to, so they could catch their breath. That didn't work.

One of my players said, Oh *no coach, I'm not going to foul out. We have twelve players; you won't foul out.*
Then the other players started saying, We *don't want to foul out either.*

I knew I was in trouble because it was only the start of the second quarter. So, I spoke to the referee about our league.

In our league, when a team is losing by a certain amount, we let the clock run.
Oh no, coach. When the whistle blows, we must stop the clock.
At the end of the game, one of my players said, *I know how they won; they were cheating.*
The final score was 108-8.
I said, *If they were called for cheating for 50 points, we would still have lost by 50.*

The kids were crying; the parents who drove over were mad. However, we still displayed good sportsmanship by shaking hands at the end of the game. We loaded the bus to start our ride back to Ocean City.

I remembered what Eric had instructed me to do—drive straight over and straight back. It was a sad time for the players. I felt bad because I thought I had prepared the team, and then it happened—losing by 100 points!

> One of the players asked, *Coach, has anyone ever lost by 100 points in this tournament?*
> *No, I don't think so.*
> His follow-up: *Did we break a record?*
> *I guess so.*

The kids started singing at the top of their lungs. *We broke a record. Hey! We broke a record. Hey! We broke a record.* People stared out their windows at us while they were driving down the street. The kids were so happy that when one player asked, *Coach, can we stop at McDonald's?* —sensing I might be fired anyway—I said yes, then pulled in even though I was supposed to drive straight back.

When we arrived at Ocean City, the kids got off the bus singing and the parents asked,

> *Hondo, what did you do to these kids to lift their spirits?*
> I said, *All I know is that they broke a record.*

At 8:30 the next morning, I told my friend Ron Rickards that we lost by 100 points. He said, *Lets go, Hondo. We need to go prepare the fields for softball play.*

> At lunch, Ron came rushing toward me and said, *Hondo, I heard you lost by 100 points last night!*
> *Yes, I told you that at 8:30 this morning.*
> *I didn't believe you.*

If you Google *Give Hondo a Hand*, you will see an article about the game in *Park and Rec Business.*

CHAPTER 28

MOOSE HOLLAND'S BOAT RIDE— NEVER. AGAIN.

There were always repairs and improvements needed on the 4th Street ball fields. One morning, Ron and I were pounding metal stakes into the ground with a post hole digger. We then attached fencing along the outfield. That afternoon was reserved for preparing the field for evening league play.

Our schoolmate, Moose Holland, steered up to the ball field bulkhead in his boat and shouted,

Why don't you guys take a break and take a ride in my boat?
I said to Ron, *I don't want to take a ride. I have never really liked boat rides; they involve too much water for me.*
Ron said, *We are at work and we can't leave. Besides, it's almost lunchtime.*
Moose replied, *Why don't you take your lunchtime and ride with me?*

We agreed, although I was shaking as I climbed down the bulkhead into his boat. Everything seemed fine—until we pulled away. I could see Moose was excited about his boat.

He asked, *How do you like my boat?*
It's nice; how long have you had it?
I've had it for a while, but I just got it back.
I looked at Ron and he looked at me.

I asked, *What do you mean, you just got it back?*
You see these round marks in the bottom of the boat?
I looked down and all I could see was all these round marks in the bottom of the boat.
It just got repaired. All those marks were holes in the bottom of the boat that've just been plugged. See? No leaks!

I immediately became nervous. I could feel my heart beating faster.

I said, *Moose, please take me back.*

By that time, we were approaching the Route 90 Bridge, about fifty-seven blocks away from the ball fields. He and Ron began to laugh. I almost started shaking. Moose agreed to turn the boat around, and we headed back. I couldn't wait to see the ball field. As we cruised closer and closer to the ball field bulkhead, I got even more nervous. I was about to panic.

I kept thinking, *The moment I get close enough, I'm getting out.* I didn't want to take any chance that he might take me back out. Once I saw the bottom of the water, I jumped out of the boat. I walked the rest of the way, striding through the water. I stepped on the first rocks at the shore and out of the water. I climbed up and over the bulkhead and onto the ball field. I was so relieved. Ron and Moose couldn't stop laughing.

Moose said, *Hondo I was going to get you closer so you wouldn't have to get wet.*
That's okay; I don't mind getting wet.

I now laugh at that experience, but I still have nightmares. All those holes in the bottom of that boat…I just didn't feel safe.

CHAPTER 29
PING-PONG COMPETITON

We loved the ping-pong table at O.C. Recreation & Parks. I believe it was donated to the department. I do know that it got plenty of use—not only by participants, but by employees as well. Greg and I started a ping-pong competition after work. Some of our very best ping-pong competition took place then. We looked forward to our own recreation. We were responsible for locking up the center at night, so after we secured everything, it was *game on*. We played every night before heading home, but sometimes we played at lunch or in the morning before work. Ping-pong, or table tennis as it is sometimes called, was a great way to relieve some stress. Although we were in the recreation business, we were both competitive when it came to ping-pong. We would play two, three, or four games, depending on the time we had. It was just something that fostered good morale between employees. Ron and Kevin also played at times. Although we remained competitive, playing ping-pong was always fun.

CHAPTER 30
MY SOFTBALL UMPIRING CAREER

While I kept score for softball, I met many umpires. As I watched the techniques they used, I couldn't help but think *I can do that*. Umpiring was a set of skills that could be learned by repeating strategies and techniques. Of course, good judgment was essential. I remember an umpire named Gary asking me if I would be interested in becoming an umpire; I told him I wasn't sure. He shared that a new umpire association was being formed and they were looking for new umpires.

I thought about it for a few days and decided to give him a call. Besides, I needed the extra money. I could umpire on the nights that I wasn't keeping score. I attended the umpires' meeting at the Wicomico Civic Center in Salisbury, Maryland. I really needed some training. I was assigned some slow-pitch softball scrimmages to gain some knowledge. After a few games of learning the basic rules, I felt good about umpiring. Both experienced umpires and newcomers joined the Delmarva Umpires Association.

My first assignment was a game in Salisbury, Maryland. When I arrived, I was so nervous. I faced a new field, new players, and a new environment. I kept looking for the other umpire. I noticed how the players were warming up; something seemed different. The game was about to start. I seemed to be the only umpire who showed up. Just before the game started, the number one home plate umpire in the association showed up. I was so relieved. Still nervous but with my partner behind the plate, I felt good. *Everything should go well for my first game.* I didn't anticipate any problems.

When the game started, I noticed that the pitcher was not pitching in a slow pitch manner. He was throwing the pitch as fast as he could. I kept wondering why he was pitching that way. The first player walked. I took my position behind first base in preparation for the next batter. Well, before I could blink, the batter on first base took off. He sprinted away to steal second base. In slow pitch, the runner can't leave the base until the batter hits the ball. I was completely out of position.

The players from both teams started yelling at me. *That is your call! What are you doing at first base?* I thought my partner, behind home plate, would have my back.

However, he also yelled out, *What the heck are you doing?*
I called time out and ran over to him.
He said, *You were not in the correct position to make that call. You're making me look bad.*
I said, *You're right. That's because I've never been trained to umpire fastpitch. The association only trained me for slow pitch.*
He was so upset with me.
I said, *It's not my fault. You must help me with my positioning for this game.*

He didn't like it, but he helped me. We survived that game. That was my last fastpitch game.

I was not going to be embarrassed again. I contacted the umpire's association and made that clear. The next game was in Pittsville, Maryland. I always understood Pittsville to be an area that I needed to be very careful in. I don't think the race relations back then were very good. I had been informed by friends that I should not be in Pittsville alone; I went anyway. I showed up early, hoping to go over the rules with the other umpire. I didn't want any mix-ups like what happened at my last game. I also wanted to inform the other ump that the training I had completed was on the bases and not behind the plate. It was about thirty minutes before the game was to start. All umpires should have arrived at the field by then.

I parked way down the left-field line. I watched the players warm up. With fifteen minutes to go, I began to get very nervous. This was only my second game, and the umpire was late again. I started praying that he would show up. I had only umpired the bases. I had only tried to umpire from behind the plate in the practice scrimmages. That hadn't gone well. I didn't want to call balls and strikes. It was five minutes before the game, and there was still no umpire.

The coordinator for the field shouted, *Has anyone seen the umpires?*
The players all shouted, *No, not yet!*

I crouched way down in my car. I didn't want anyone to see me. I wanted to start my car and leave. If I could have backed my car out, I would have. But since I was dressed to umpire, someone would have spotted me. So, I just kept quiet and hoped for the best. Then my worst nightmare came true.

One of the players hollered, *There he is—he's right here! The umpire is here! We can get started*

I realized that the other umpire was not going to show. I had to do two things I had never done before: umpire by myself and umpire from behind the plate.

But I still realized I was in Pittsville. That made me nervous all over again. I got out of my car and walked over to the coordinator. I explained my circumstances, admitting that I had no experience umpiring from behind the plate. I think the players could sense that I was nervous, but they didn't say anything at the time. The coordinator called the captains to home plate to explain, and I couldn't believe it. Each team had a captain who was towering over me at about 6'4". At a stretch, I measure 5'5".

Somebody was surely looking out for me. When I looked up, I realized that I had gone to college with both.

I told them I had never been behind the plate. They were so nice. They both said, *Hondo don't worry about it, just do the best you can.*

I felt better after that. However, once I said *Play ball!* things went crazy. I called a strike on the first pitch. Both benches emptied and players came running from the dugouts. One team was complaining that I called the pitch a strike. The other team was saying *You can't change that call!* My heart was beating so fast. This went on for about three minutes, which seemed like ten minutes to me. Before I could say anything, they all fell to the ground laughing at me. Can you imagine being surrounded by about twenty guys on the ground laughing at the same time? Then they stopped and both team captains said, *Hondo, we couldn't help it. We knew you were nervous. We couldn't resist playing a joke on you.* I was so happy. I thought the game was going to be a nightmare.

I decided that I was going to do the best one-man umpiring job I could. I wasn't nervous anymore. I would race down to first base ahead of the batters to call them out. I would beat players to the second base to make a call. I took the correct angle to make calls at third and home plate. At the end of the game, all the players complimented me on my hustle. But they didn't like fact that I beat them to the bases. As I drove home, I shouted *I will never do a one-man system again* loud enough for other drivers to hear me. I made sure the umpires association's assignor knew that the other umpire didn't show up. I never quit anything that I started, although I had wanted to that night. I finished out the umpiring season that summer but hung up my cleats after that year.

CHAPTER 31

WHAT YOU GOT GOING?!

Earlier I mentioned that Gerald Groves was my first Recreation & Parks Director at City Hall. Our staff gave him many nicknames over the years, but none was more significant than *The Big Cheese*. I believe we gave him so many nicknames because we loved him so much. He really enjoyed working with us and he changed our department for the better. There was a routine he became known for with the staff. His office was on the second floor over the gymnasium. We could hear him coming down the stairs each morning. He would approach us and ask, *What you got going?* It was his way of finding out what was on our agenda for the day. Because he asked us this so many times, we came up with a name for him. Rather than referring to him as the boss, we decided on *The Big Cheese*. We always had a good laugh each morning about that. I'm not sure that he liked it at first. However, once some of his staff started calling him just *Cheese*, he just accepted it. It has been forty years since we started calling him Cheese and we still do it. He is known by two names: the community calls him Gerry, but some of us still call him *The Big Cheese*.

CHAPTER 32

THE 3RD STREET GYMNASIUM

The 3rd Street Basketball Courts saw a lot of basketball games, but those courts couldn't be compared to the indoor court. The most popular place to recreate indoors was the 3rd Street Gymnasium. If you got to play indoors at City Hall in the early '80s, you were on top of the world. The gymnasium had been part of the Ocean City School. Back in 1917, the school was for both elementary and high school students. The first floor was for elementary students, and the high school students' classes were on the second floor. Ocean City School won a Maryland Class C State Basketball Championship in 1952. The school closed after 38 years.

Sometime much later, the gymnasium began to be used for youth and adult recreation. The gymnasium can in no way be compared to the gymnasiums at Northside Park. With the government's safety regulations of today, it would not meet many standards. But it was all we had. When you shot a layup at one end of the court, you had to prepare yourself to bounce off the brick wall. The wall was only about three feet from the end line. We eventually put up mats to help prevent injuries. The side out-of-bounds lines were about six inches from the wall, with an eyehook sticking out of the wall for volleyball. We had to crawl across the beams in the ceilings to change light bulbs. Despite all the challenges, we still loved playing in that gym.

During men's and women's basketball leagues, that gymnasium was packed with spectators. It was the place to be during the week. The kids loved the gym.

Suellen Vickers was the first girl to play in the youth boys basketball league. Suellen was a fantastic athlete—head and shoulders above all the other girls. She went on to receive a basketball scholarship at the University of Maryland. I remember Allison Harman, a co-worker, played on one of the two girls' teams we had.

The 3rd Street Gymnasium also offered volleyball for adults. Baseball was practiced inside when it rained. With the wood floors, a roller-skating program was offered. I would unlock the gym doors on Sundays for drop-in basketball. At lunchtime, public works employees would stop by to shoot baskets. There would be about ten sanitation trucks parked along 3rd Street each weekday at noon. The 3rd Street Gymnasium was a great place where employees could recreate every day of the week.

When we started the Over 30 Basketball League, nearly all City Hall employees played. A citywide league drew players from public works, the police department, and, of course, players from the local businesses. When we decided that the courts needed a three-point line, we did that paint job in-house. That made the league even more popular.

Here are a few notable participants in the Over 30 league: Dennis Dare, Gerald Groves, Greg Purnell, Ron Rickards, Rich Currence, Robert Mumford, John Vanfossen, Steve Pappas, Mike Donahue, Pete Wimbrow, Thom Lord Tom Dickerson, Bobby Vermillion, Doc Duval, Ray Land, Quinton (Boo Peep) Dennis, and Chris Sheridan.

CHAPTER 33

THE END OF WOMEN'S SOFTBALL

Ocean City Women's Softball exemplified what recreation was all about. It didn't matter how bright the sun was shining or how hot the 3rd Street and 4th Street sidewalks were; people lined up to watch the games. On Monday and Wednesday, people came off the beach to witness some fantastic play by these restaurant-sponsored teams. They were one of the main attractions downtown.

Our director, Gerald Groves—affectionately known as Cheese—had done so many things for our department. He was featured on the front page of the National Recreation & Parks Association (NRPA) Magazine, representing Ocean City. He also attended Maryland Recreation Parks Association (MRPA) meetings and NRPA Conferences to learn about new programs and innovations in recreation.

Once, Cheese returned from a conference and had this great idea. He loved softball. We had the Tuesday/Thursday Men's League, the Sunday Men's League, and the Women's League. Now he wanted to start a Co-ed League. His goal was to increase participation in softball since it was one of our most popular programs.

The next summer, he set up a meeting for the Co-ed Softball League. It was well attended. I think it looked like we were going to have an additional league. We had a very competitive Women's Softball League for many years. However, when it was time for the Women's Softball meeting that year, no one showed up. The Co-ed League had most of the same

players, so the Women's League came to an end. Most women probably didn't want to play in both leagues. Summer work probably wouldn't
allow it anyway. Co-ed Softball did thrive and continued to grow for the
next few years.

CHAPTER 34

EARL THE PEARL SOFTBALL RULE

Downtown, softball had a well-known character who was always around: Earl Austin. Earl The Pearl, as we called him, was a Pearl Harbor Survivor. I am not sure when he came to Ocean City, but everyone knew Earl. He was a man who really enjoyed life. Earl also enjoyed softball. He was a pitcher for Pete Wimbrow's Bar Fly Softball Team. He couldn't play any other position because he had a bad leg.

Before I continue talking about Earl, I must explain why everyone liked him so much. Remember when I said he enjoyed life? Well, what I really meant—Earl could be very entertaining. If he was not playing softball that day or that night, he would come to the field anyway. Earl would harass all the opposing softball players, but none of them paid him any mind. At first, I couldn't understand how he got to the field with his bad leg, and then I found out that he only lived a block away. There were a few nights when the games were over that I helped him. I would walk or drive Earl to his house, then help him get inside.

Because of Earl's bad leg, I added the Earl the Pearl Rule to our softball rules. Earl could still bat and—most of the time—get a hit. The problem was he couldn't run—he could barely walk. The rule was that a player on the bench would position himself behind the plate. He could only run after Earl contacted the ball. In other words, we would have a designated runner for Earl. No one complained about the rule; they were just glad to see a Pearl Harbor Survivor playing in our league.

CHAPTER 35

PETE WIMBROW—4TH STREET COURT REBOUNDING KING

Pete Wimbrow was a great supporter of our Recreation & Parks Department from behind the scenes—a long-time basketball enthusiast with lots of knowledge about the game. He also loved softball. Each year, Pete would organize the local attorneys to play on his softball team. We were supposed to have a limit to the number of players on a team. However, Pete would always have a long list of lawyers. His team didn't win very many games. But they would always show up to play. Pete had teams for many years, especially when we played downtown on the 4th Street Softball Field. He also played when we moved to 125th Street at Northside Park.

Pete's passion was really basketball. He would pay the league fee for basketball teams he didn't even play on. When he played on the 4th Street Basketball Courts, he was in his own world. He stood 6'4" or 6'5" and weighed probably 250 or more. He was a very physical specimen. His long strides got him down the court, but not very fast. His specialty was rebounding and defense. I don't even think he cared about scoring. He really enjoyed rebounding. There have been many high school, college, and professional basketball players who have played on the 4th Street courts. I don't think anyone has played as many games on those courts as Pete. I have played on those courts many times, but not as much as Pete has. Pete guarded many top collegiate and NBA big men on 4th Street. He was so proud of the courts—so much so that when the town was thinking about moving or changing the courts, Pete spoke up in support of keeping the courts just as they were.

Pete's favorite basketball player was Wilt Chamberlain, the NBA's All-Time Leading Rebounder. Wilt and Pete had something in common. Wilt was the NBA's leading rebounder and Pete is known as the All-Time Leading Rebounder on 4th Street. In fact, if you visit Pete's office, you will see a picture of the two together. Pete has many stories about playing on 4th Street. Many other basketball players support the 4th Street courts, but Pete is the leading advocate for those basketball courts.

CHAPTER 36

SOFTBALL SCOREKEEPING ON ST. LOUIS AVENUE

Sometimes an opportunity just falls in your lap. In 1981, Director Groves—Cheese— asked me if I would be a scorekeeper for the men's softball league. I needed to think about that at first. The job was after my eight-hour day job, but the opportunity would provide me a chance to earn extra money, so I accepted the job. I would be scorekeeper for the Tuesday/Thursday Softball League. I often think about the number of times I have said or written down that league name to start a game. There were about ten to twelve teams in the league, with restaurants, bars, businesses, and other organizations serving as local sponsors.

My job was supposed to be keeping score behind home plate. This allowed me to sit in the bleachers to watch every play. Well, Cheese didn't tell me I had to retrieve the home run and foul balls. The ball field was next to the very busy St. Louis Avenue. Cars constantly drove past the field. Cars would get hit by foul balls from time to time. When that happened, I was charged with writing up the incident report, sometimes with the police involved. Softballs would be hit into the skate park, which was the next block over. I had to unlock the skate park to locate the softballs—in the dark. I had to do all of this while keeping score.

I also had to run down St. Louis Avenue to locate softballs. After a while, I would just get the game lineups and head down St. Louis Avenue to keep score. I would ask the left fielder for each team to let me know what each batter did. After all, I was almost three hundred feet away from the home plate and the umpire.

Just behind the left-field line homerun fence was a house owned by Roger Steager's family. When I knew a homerun hitting team was batting, I would take a glove and stand in front of his house. Sometimes his children would be playing in his yard. Homerun balls would bounce in his yard. When he was there, he would keep the balls. I remember that he took a bucket of balls or two to a city council meeting to complain. Not long after that, a large net was put up to help prevent the balls from going into his yard. I still think a few made it over the net. That net is still there after more than forty years.

After I accepted the job as Tuesday/Thursday scorekeeper, I was asked to keep score for the Sunday Softball League. The league played in both Ocean City and at Ocean City Elementary School. This gave me another opportunity to meet so many more players, many who are still living in Ocean City today. Sometime in the future, there will be a Softball Hall of Fame. My first inductees would be Thom Lord, Ron Rickards, Moose Holland, Dave "Littleman" Cropper, Mark Mitchell, Larry Handy, Johnny Watson, Phil Fort, Kevin Hudson, and Dave Hudson.

CHAPTER 37

THE DUCKS ARE LITTLE LEAGUE CHAMPS

Having played baseball in high school, college, and as a semi-pro, I loved baseball as much as I loved life itself. I had a chance to teach kids in Ocean City the basics of the game. I was excited to provide them with new drills to improve their skills, all while having fun.

My first-year team was the Ducks; we were in the league for ages 8-12. So, you might imagine the different body frames of the kids both short and tall. But it didn't matter. We still enjoyed ourselves.

Coach Wayne Littleton and I enjoyed coaching the team. Although we won the championship three years in a row, that wasn't what we wanted to focus on. We wanted to have the players learn what good sportsmanship was. We always encouraged our players. We were happy to know that our players went on to become great citizens.

I wanted to see what some of the players felt, some forty years later. We coached Scott Hands, Trevor Steadman, Jay Yilmaz, Chad Vent, Malcolm VanKirk, Chris Shaffer, Damion Lanza, Bunky Hensler, Andrew Hobbs, Eric Podowski, Joe Dezarn, Brian and Adam Winter, Elias and Demetris Zacharopoulos, to name a few. I was able to reach three of our former players who are now living all over the country: Bunky Hensler, Chad Vent, and Jay Yilmaz. I asked them about their baseball experience with us. Their comments are below.

BUNKY HENSLER

Looking back, I can easily say that the pinnacle of my youth sports days came at the ripe old age of eight, playing for the OC Ducks and Coach Al Handy, AKA "Hondo." Yeah, it was the only championship team that I ever played on. But that's not the real reason that I look so fondly back to that season.

It was my very first season playing baseball. It's where I learned to play the sport. It's where I developed my love for the sport, the patience and respect for the sport. The sportsmanship we learned from Coach Handy and Coach Littleton has stuck with me my whole life. We practiced at the ball field on 3rd Street and, when the weather was bad, we took it indoors at City Hall. I vividly remember first learning to slide correctly on the slick floors of City Hall. Fundamentals were key. We all benefited immensely from Coach Handy's focus on them as the building blocks of greater things to come… Again, I was 8 years old, and a small 8-year-old at that.

My strike zone at the plate was about the size of a shoebox. There was no T-ball or coach pitch league. I played on an 8-12-year-old team—the championship OC Ducks under head coach Al Handy…*Best beginning to playing sports that anyone could ever wish for!*

CHAD VENT

Albin "Hondo" Handy was my first Little League coach, and he did not disappoint! I can vividly recall the smile and enthusiasm Coach Hondo would show up with to every practice and game; because of this, I always looked forward to the next one. I grew up in the gyms of the OC Recreation Department. Hondo was always there with the same positive demeanor. His positivity influenced thousands of kids who went through the OC Recreation Department. As an adult, when I see him around now, I immediately smile and am thankful for the role he played in my life. *Hondo truly has been a beacon for me.*

JOSEPH A. "JAY" YILMAZ, FREEPORT, ME.

Looking back on the special time in one's youth, I could not be more thankful—thankful for the very good luck that my Little League teammates and I had as members of *The Ducks*. Our team, sponsored by The Donald Duck Shoppe, had probably been brought together randomly. Most importantly, we were aligned with Coach Al Handy, the man who came to be affectionately known as Hondo.

I must believe that we had the best coach who ever drew a breath—the best coach of all time, from here to the Moon and back. I hope that, for the sake of one's sacred time as a youth, every young person has had someone in their life who has been so kind...someone as inspiring as Coach Handy was for us as impressionable young boys.

Within a year or two, Hondo gained an assistant who we came to know as Coach Wayne. As if the tone or mood could not have been better under Hondo's tutelage, the dynamic between Coach Wayne and Coach Handy was amazing. They inspired our sandlot bunch to play our best. They taught us the love of the game which will always remain in our hearts. Though we didn't realize it at the time being young kids, it is easy to see as an adult that Coaches Hondo and Wayne imparted all the important core values that one would hope could be instilled in their child. They were very kind, gentle, generous, and decent men who set a high bar for our team. They carried themselves in such a way that none of the players would have wanted to disappoint our coaches, on or off the field.

As a testament to the generosity and kindness of Coach Handy, I remember one day that he pulled me aside after watching me struggle for a season or maybe two with a glove that was never properly broken in. I recall that playing catch with that glove was not easy; in fact, it was quite a drag—like trying to catch with a plastic cup. This certainly did not help the confidence of the smallest guy on the team. To my surprise, Coach Handy offered me with one of his soft, well-worn, and perfectly seasoned gloves. It almost seemed ready to catch the ball by itself. It certainly allowed me to enjoy my experience and probably made me a better player, if only by boosting my confidence. Incidentally, I wrote to Coach in 2009 to thank him for his kindness and to let him know that my son was using that same glove!

Another gesture of kindness that Coach showed me was when I was in fourth grade. We were performing *Casey at the Bat.* We needed baseball uniforms, but the teacher (coincidentally, Mrs. Casey) was stumped at how to gather thirty uniforms since not everyone played baseball. I had an idea that I mentioned to my mom: *How about asking Coach Handy if we could borrow some Recreation Department Baseball uniforms?* She encouraged me to contact him, which was perhaps my first foray into making connections. It turned out to be one of my strengths, greater than my prowess with a baseball. Coach was very generous and willing to allow the uniforms to be loaned to me and our class, especially since it was during winter and before baseball season.

We owe a great debt of gratitude to Coaches Hondo and Wayne for the wonderful memories and life lessons. For me, having Hondo as my first coach will remain one of the fondest memories of my youth. *Just like there's only that one guy who you call "Dad," Hondo is that one guy who will always be "Coach" to me.*

CHAPTER 38

MEETING BROOKS ROBINSON

I was a big Baltimore Orioles fan. My favorite players were the Robinson Brothers, Brooks and Frank. I couldn't believe Brooks was coming to Ocean City! Many people may not remember, but the Baltimore Orioles were World Series Champions in 1983. Not long after that, one of their stars, Brooks, and pitching coach Billy Hunter came to Ocean City to do a clinic on the 4th Street ball fields.

Ron Rickards and I had the pleasure of assisting them that day. They brought excitement to the youth in our community. I believe the owner of Mug & Mallet, Mr. Ken Grau, and a local radio station had sponsored the Orioles duo to come down. The clinic lasted about an hour; it was followed by a photo op and some autographs. It was a great opportunity for our local kids to see a professional baseball player up close.

It was an honor for me and Ron to be on hand for such as special occasion. I also took a picture with Brooks Robinson; it hung in my bedroom for several years. I will never forget meeting Brooks and Coach Hunter.

CHAPTER 39

THE SUNFEST
SOFTBALL TOURNAMENT

If you were a softball player, you heard about the Sunfest Softball Tournament in Ocean City, Maryland. Players arrived with $300 bats, team uniforms with $200 price tags, and expensive softball gloves. With so many teams, the games had to start early Saturday morning.

Playing softball games at 8:00 a.m. meant preparing the fields around 6:30 a.m. This would give the teams time to warm up. Sometimes the fields were not closed until 1:00 a.m. Sunday morning, only to start again at 8:00 a.m. There were not many softball tournaments on the Eastern Shore in the '80s. This tournament became one of the most popular softball tournaments on the East Coast. It was not just a weekend for the players; it was also for their families. Players came from up and down the East Coast to compete. Some of the best softball players in the nation participated. Many players had to fly in. It was an exciting time for Ocean City and softball fans.

The tournament expanded from sixteen to thirty-two teams during Director Groves' tenure. I asked Gerry what he remembers about the tournament. His response:

I remember expanding the tournament, doing a draw at Shenanigans, and no new teams could get in unless they would bid. It was during this time that we started selling t-shirts. I do remember one year, due to rain, we went to a one-pitch rule to get the games in. This meant that each pitch was a hit, a strike-out, or a walk to help speed the tournament up. That weekend, we played until 4:00 a.m. I don't think the neighbors were very happy.

We played on ball fields in downtown Ocean City at 4th Street, West Ocean City, the Showell Ball Fields, and later at Northside Park. We used to let the softball players just hit them high and let them fly—another way to say we let the hitters hit as many home runs as they could. We moved to the fields at Northside, and the scoreboards there had sirens. They were used every time a homerun was hit. The loud sirens were exciting for the spectators and the players. Players from the other fields knew whenever a home run was hit. I don't think the neighbors liked the sirens.

On Friday nights, teams would travel to Ocean City for the draw party. The team representative would pick a softball that told them what time they played their first game. When Tom Perlozzo became the director, we moved the tournament drawing party closer to Northside. The draw was held at places like the Ocean Club, The Greene Turtle, and Hooters. Some of the local teams that won over the years were the Bull on the Beach, Purple Moose, and Charlie's Tuna.

Toward the end of my participation in this tournament, not only were the top men's softball players in the nation playing—the tournament drew some of the top players in the world. It was a two-day tournament that drew large crowds and brought a lot of revenue to Ocean City.

CHAPTER 40

OCEAN CITY'S ALL-AROUND ATHLETE, RON "ICE MAN" RICKARDS

History will show that the best athlete ever to participate in Ocean City Recreation & Parks Programs is Ron Rickards. Ron earned several nicknames throughout his career. Rooster—or the Ice Man, as we called him—would be a First Ballot Hall of Famer if Ocean City had one. I can't remember how he got the name Rooster, but Ice Man came because he was a deadeye three-point shooter on the basketball court.

I have known Ron since we were in high school. He was one of the fastest athletes ever at Stephen Decatur High. He grew up in Berlin playing all sorts of sports such as basketball, soccer, and football. But it seemed his best sport was baseball. He played on my high school baseball team when I was a senior. As a freshman, he led the team in homeruns. How's that for skill at such a young age?

I got the opportunity to become a baseball coach for Salisbury State College; that was not on my radar. But I got a chance to play with and coach my old teammate, Ron Rickards, at Salisbury. It is hard to imagine. What a great experience for me.

I was hoping to go to the next level. So, what happened at a Baltimore Orioles tryout one summer? All players had to sprint to show how fast they were. There were hundreds of players there. What happened? My race partner just happened to be none other than Ron Rickards. I won't tell you who won our race. That's between us. I will tell you that I think he could have played professionally.

I moved to Harford County, then back to Ocean City—and took a job at the Recreation & Parks Department. Who do I see on my first day at the job? My good friend and teammate, Ron, was employed there also!

Ron was not only a great baseball player; he could really shoot the basketball. When it came to the men's basketball league; he was the player to stop. He was deadly from the three-point line. If you raced out to guard him, he was so fast that he would just go in for a lay-up.

On the football field, he could anticipate passes for interceptions and race back the length of the field to score. A deep threat on offense, he had hands like magnets and the speed to outrun his opponents.

After baseball, Ron took up softball. I will never forget the bond between him and his father on the softball field. His mother was always there to support him, too. At every game, his ability to catch, throw, play defense, hit singles, doubles, triples, and homeruns was on full display. He was known for making the big play.

Fellow teammates really respected him. Athletes in Ocean City would agree if they were ranking overall talent, Ron would be number one. His many awards, honors, and championships exemplified his "Best All Around" status.

CHAPTER 41

MY DREAM JOB—BECOMING A RECREATION SPECIALIST

When you put in the work, get the education, and receive your degree—you never know when your dream job will materialize. While I truly enjoyed being the first public grounds specialist for the Town of Ocean City, it was *not* my dream position. My dream came true in 1985. I remember it like it was yesterday. At the time I was still very dedicated to the Parks Division as the public grounds specialist. I had just helped Ocean City win their first Tree City USA Award. Our parks building was now located at beautiful Northside Park. The park was rated by many, near and far, as the best park in Maryland.

My co-worker Tracy and I were headed to Salisbury to pick up a delivery of flowers for the beautification of our parks when across our radio comes a loud voice: *Base to Hondo!* Tracy and I looked at each other because we knew it was our director, Tom Perlozzo. We wondered what was wrong: Was I was in trouble?

I suddenly felt a lump in my throat as I answered, *Go ahead; this is Hondo.*
Our director said, *What's your twenty?*—meaning *where are you?*

Nervousness set in, but I knew my supervisor, Calvin, was aware that we were heading out of town.

I responded, *We are headed to Salisbury to pick up our delivery of flowers.*

To make things even worse, his response was only *See me when you get back.*

The way he said it made me worry even more. All my co-workers in the Parks Division could also hear him on the radio. I could just hear them saying to each other, *What has Hondo done?*

We hadn't even gotten to Salisbury yet. That meant we had to think about his comments the rest of the way to Salisbury and all the way back to the office. What could it be? We could not think of anything we had done wrong. Since you didn't get called into his office often, we both assumed the worst. We had signed out, informed our supervisor, informed the front office, then filled our truck with gas and headed to Salisbury. We did everything by the book.

I decided that I should go into the office as soon as I got back. When I got to Northside Park, I stopped at the front desk.

I said, *Tom wants to see me.*

The front office staff said, *Yes, he does want to see you; go back to his office.*

This was a long, slow walk for me. It was only about twenty feet, but it seemed much longer because of the pace I was keeping. With my heart beating twice as fast as normal, I knocked on his door.

Come in, close the door, and take a seat.

I said to myself, *Oh no!* I knew everyone was waiting to hear what happened, including Tracy, who was waiting for me.

Are you still interested in working with the Program Division?

Yes of course.

Well, congratulations, you are going to be our newest recreation specialist.

I did not know what to say at first. I just said, *Thank you for the opportunity!*

Some time ago, I had met with Tom and expressed my interest in becoming a recreation specialist. I really wanted to work with kids. I knew that was my calling. That call on the radio to come see him had made me so nervous. The thought of getting my dream job that day never crossed my mind, but that is how my recreation career got started. I have never been happier in my life. That day changed my life forever. I learned so much from Tom and I will be forever grateful.

Throughout my career my title changed from Recreation Specialist to Recreation Programmer to Recreation Supervisor. Before I retired, I had become a recreation manager along with my co-worker, Kim Kinsey. I had many responsibilities including supervising as many as fifty part-time staff and hundreds of volunteers throughout the years. I would not even think about putting a number on how many participants were in our programs. I will only say that I have been in direct contact with thousands.

I was also responsible for the concession's operations and Ocean City Tennis Operation. I secured sponsors for our youth programs, worked as a liaison between the department and community organizations, was a guest speaker at many community meetings, served on several committees including the All-American City; Ocean City Drug & Alcohol Abuse Prevention Committee; the Play It Safe Committee; Maryland Recreation & Parks Association's Membership Committee and the National Alliance for Youth Sports Advisory Board. I served as Ocean City Little League Baseball president and Ocean City Pony League Baseball president. I served as the department lead for the National Youth Sports Coach Association, later to be named the National Alliance for Youth Sports.

My duties changed, but the goal was still the same: to provide quality recreation programming for the locals and our visitors. Our mission was to provide quality recreational, cultural, and social opportunities, as well as safe, clean, enjoyable parks, beaches, and facilities to enhance the quality of life for Ocean City residents and visitors…something that could not have been done without the help of everyone in our department, the city departments, and of course the mayor and members of City Council.

To say I didn't enjoyed every day that I came to work would be an untrue statement. To say that every day I started with a smiling face and ended with a smiling face would be true. I did not want my co-workers, my staff, my supervisor, or our participants to know that I ever had a bad day. I learned early that if you don't look like you are enjoying yourself, the kids and parents will pick up on that right away. That goes for the adult participants also. There are so many programs that I was involved with, responsible for, created, piloted, or supervised. I truly enjoyed my time working with all the recreation programs and the community.

CHAPTER 42
ANNUAL YOUTH AWARDS BANQUET

For many years, the program year ended with the Ocean City Recreation and Parks Youth Awards Banquet. Seeing the entire community come together each year to celebrate the achievements of our youth gave me such a great feeling. The smiling faces of those kids meant so much to me.

The event started at the Ocean City Convention Center, then moved to Northside Park. Director Perlozzo invited guest speakers such as Bobby McAvan of the Indoor Soccer Champion Baltimore Blast, Gary Clark of the World Champion Washington Redskins, Bill Robinson of the New York Mets, and Greg Manusky of the Washington Redskins—all professional athletes at the time. I remember picking the guest speakers up from their hotels and bringing them to our event. Of course, I would get a photo with them.

All the sports teams were recognized. All the children received awards for their yearlong accomplishments. We even had food catered for the banquet. It seemed like every kid in Ocean City and the surrounding area attended. It was a lot of work, but well worth it. Participants from our Youth Soccer Leagues, Boys and Girls Basketball Leagues, Little League Baseball Leagues and clinics gathered for a day of food, fun, and socialization.

We would hold a separate awards day for our sponsors. Taking their photos was a personal touch for the community. We awarded our businesses and community organizations with nice plaques. If they didn't attend the banquet, we would deliver the plaques.

CHAPTER 43

THE GRAND OPENING OF THE NORTHSIDE PARK BALL FIELDS AND SOCCER FIELDS

SOFTBALL FIELDS

A very proud moment for me and our city was the grand opening of the Northside Park Ball Fields. Director Perlozzo invited Berlin Little League over to play our Little League Baseball teams. One of our Little Leaguers, Steve Andrews, threw out the first pitch to open the Northside Ball fields, I believe.

It was not only a great day for Ocean City, but everyone from the nearby Town of Berlin got to see the new fields. We even had our concessions open. It was also an introduction to the entire park. Many locals were used to downtown recreation on 3rd Street. Many people, especially from West Ocean City and Berlin, had never taken the take the trip to 125th Street.

Our programs, such as the Tuesday/Thursday Softball League, the Sunday Softball League, and the Co-Rec Softball League, started using the fields. But soon, requests to use the ball fields started to come. Stephen Decatur High School organizers for softball tournaments and lacrosse tournaments were requesting use of the fields. We held events such as the Fourth of July Jamboree on the fields and in the park. The park soon became one of the most popular parks in the state of Maryland.

LIGHTED SOCCER FIELD

The Grand Opening for the soccer field was a big deal. Soccer was big in Ocean City, so there was lots of press for the event. The game featured the Ocean City All-Stars (sponsored by Greene Turtle) against the Baltimore Blast Legends. The Baltimore Blast was an indoor soccer team that went on to win the Indoor World Championship. Our soccer camp director, Bobby McAvan, was a member of the Blast and was able to bring several members from that team to Ocean City. Before the featured game was played, a couple of youth soccer teams played. When the All-Stars Legends' game was over, the kids received autographs and got to meet some of the players. This was another fun evening for the community and the young soccer players in our area.

Thank you, Bobby McAvan, for my retirement gift—the autographed Blast Soccer Jersey from that game. I have it hanging on my wall at home.

CHAPTER 44

PRO BASEBALL CLINIC WITH COACH SAM PERLOZZO

Professional baseball clinics in our area were rare, but when the opportunity presented itself to bring one to Ocean City, I chose to move forward since baseball was popular here at the time. After discussing the idea with our director, he agreed and he suggested getting his brother, Sam Perlozzo, to come down.

He said, *Maybe he could come to Ocean City before spring baseball training begins in Florida.* Sam was a former major league baseball player who was coaching with New York Mets at the time. Some of the professional players Coach Perlozzo brought with him were John Kruger from the Phillies, Bill Robinson from the Mets, and Leo Mazzone, the pitching coach for the Braves.

Our youth baseball players enjoyed meeting and learning from the pros. They even got some signed baseball cards. I think we did the clinic for three years. Sam went on to become the head coach of the Baltimore Orioles. He is presently coaching with the Minnesota Twins.

CHAPTER 45
OCEAN CITY BREAKERS BASEBALL TEAM

Semi-pro baseball in Ocean City had never happened until Perlozzo and Bobby Vermillion helped start and develop Ocean City's first team—the Ocean City Breakers. They played in the Eastern Shore Baseball League. There were teams from Salisbury, Princess Anne, Delaware, and Virginia.

Many Ocean City players were from the South. Bobby would travel to a few of the southern baseball colleges. He recruited their best players for Ocean City. Some of the players were employed by our parks division. Others found jobs in Ocean City that would allow them to practice and play in the games.

It was an exciting time for baseball enthusiasts in Ocean City. I found myself keeping score again—sometimes late into the night because most games were doubleheaders. The Ocean City Breakers' coaches were Perlozzo, Vermillion, and Tink Bayline. The games were played on Field One, which was the only baseball field at Northside Park. The other two fields were softball fields. It was a learning experience when both the baseball and softball leagues were playing at the same time.

Softball players were mad at me because the baseballs were being fouled onto their fields. The baseball players were disappointed because the softball players wouldn't return their expensive baseballs. The foul balls from the baseball league would enter the softball fields with tremendous speed, nearly injuring the players—or sometimes the spectators. The game times for the two leagues were changed very soon to increase safety during games.

The team drew a different crowd to Northside Park than those who had watched Little League or high school teams play. The league gave college baseball players the opportunity to continue playing during the summer. One of the stars was Todd Lampman. Todd remained in the area and is currently the athletic director at Snow Hill High School.

I love baseball and was glad to play a small part of supporting the Ocean City Breakers—the history-making minor league team.

CHAPTER 46

PUT ME IN, COACH

Coaches always have a challenge trying to please every player on the bench. Ocean City once had a thriving Little League Baseball program. With the introduction of lacrosse, the baseball numbers started to decrease. We didn't have the numbers to form an in-house league, so we switched to the Pony Baseball program, which allowed us to travel. Our team played against teams from Salisbury.

I remember one game when we were playing at home against a Salisbury team. Ocean City's coach, Chris McGee, was being hounded by one of his players wanting to be put in the game. We'll call this player Joe.

Coach McGee kept telling Joe that he was going in the game.
Joe, it's only the second inning, I am going to get everyone in.
Joe's pursuit was relentless. He shouted again, *Put me in, coach.*
His mother stuck her head in the dugout and said, *Calm down, he is going to put you in.* Her son's comment was, *I paid my money just like everyone else, and I should be in the game.*

In the third inning, Salisbury was beating Ocean City *bad*. The bright part for Ocean City was that the players were making good contact with the pitcher. They had even gotten a few hits. You could tell that this wasn't Salisbury's best pitcher. But this was good for Ocean City, as we hadn't won a game. Coach McGee shouted down to Joe, who continued bugging him about getting in the game.

You're going in the game next inning, so get ready.
Alright; I will be ready.

He started looking for a helmet. He picked out his favorite bat since he would be hitting next.

Meanwhile, Salisbury decided to change pitchers. No one from Ocean City seemed to notice the change, until Ocean City's number one batter stepped up to the plate. Joe should have been on deck: he was finally going to get in the game.

Back to our number one batter. The first pitch he saw was gas, a very fast pitch for a strike. The next pitch almost hit him, causing him to go to the ground. He dropped his bat and his helmet came off. After gaining his composure, he stepped back in the batter's box only to swing and miss at the next pitch. He swung extremely late at the pitch.

You could hear Coach McGee shout, *Where's our on-deck batter?*

No one seemed to know. The next pitch crossed the plate so fast that our best hitter didn't even get to swing.

The umpire shouted, *Strike three!*
He slowly walked back to the dugout. Disappointed, he said, *That pitcher is throwing smoke.*
Coach McGee said, *That's okay; you did your best.*
The umpire shouted, *Batter up!*

But our next batter, Joe, was nowhere to be found. Coach McGee finally found Joe, at the other end of the bench, with his head down. He didn't have a helmet on or a bat in his hands.

Joe, you're up to bat.
Joe said nothing at first.
Joe it's your turn to bat. Are you going in the game? Don't you want to bat?
Coach McGee asked again, *Don't you want to bat?*

I guess not.
You mean you don't want a chance to hit?
Nope.

You see, Joe had seen the new pitcher throwing smoke at the plate. He decided that it was best that he didn't go up to the plate. The game was halted, as no other batter wanted to face the Salisbury pitcher. What is the lesson learned from this scenario? *Be careful what you wish for.*

CHAPTER 47

EXAMPLES OF BAD SPORTSMANSHIP— ALL OUT FIGHTS ON THE BASKETBALL COURTS

Promoting sportsmanship became my number one goal throughout my career. However, there were times I was disappointed in my teams when I felt they didn't display that ethic I worked so hard to instill. For example, one night when our senior citizen bus returned from Atlantic City, I decided to go inside to use the restroom before heading home.

As I entered the door, I remembered the Men's Basketball League games were being played. However, something didn't seem right—some unusual noise was coming from inside the gym. As I walked into the gym, I couldn't believe my eyes. To my surprise, there was an all-out fight occurring. Two basketball teams—one from Maryland and one from Delaware— were in a physical altercation. I saw a player I knew bleeding from being hit. I got him into the office. I asked his brother to keep him there as the player who was fighting with him might still be in the gym. The fight started after an opposing player from the Delaware team attacked him from behind. Several other players had also been fighting. We got things calmed down and basketball ended for the night.

As a result of the altercation, several players were suspended. The basketball league was also suspended, and this suspension lasted for several years.

ON THE SOFTBALL FIELD

If you know anything about Men's Slow Pitch Softball, you know that teams often mouth off. The banter is usually between two competitive teams that don't like each other. So when they play each other, they are trying to see who can bully who.

We usually had six teams playing every hour on our three fields. One night, the two top softball teams were playing each other. Everyone knew these teams didn't like each other. As league director, I decided to keep an eye on them. The last time they played, it was a close game. You could see the tension building between the teams. I could tell from the start that something might happen, so I talked to the team representatives before the game. It didn't seem to help.

I can't remember what inning it was, *but someone said something—* and all the players started running toward each other. There was a lot of pushing and shoving. The result of this encounter? A suspension of several players from each team. They didn't like it, but there were many spectators in the stands. They witnessed the incident. Fighting is not tolerated in our leagues. Several players from each team suffered the consequences.

CHAPTER 48

EXAMPLES OF GOOD SPORTSMANSHIP

I like to describe good sportsmanship through five pillars: respect; fairness; integrity; responsibility; perseverance. Respect is treating people the way you want to be treated. Fairness—don't take advantage of others. Integrity—do what you're supposed to do. Have the courage to do the right thing. Responsibility—be accountable for your choices. Perseverance—always try your best; be persistent. Have that *never give up* attitude; have a positive attitude. To be a good sport is to be a person of good character.

There are so many examples of good sportsmanship that I could mention. Most of the examples of good sportsmanship occurred during our youth programs since the participants, parents, and coaches paid attention to what we were promoting.

We emphasized good sportsmanship year-round by hanging large motivational banners in each gymnasium, providing sportsmanship information in the parent packages, and giving participants glow-in-the-dark *Sportsmanship counts!* wristbands. We ended our programs each night with the kids getting together to do a big *One, two, three…Sportsmanship counts!* shout – out so the parents could hear our closing message.

I started the Ocean City Sportsmanship Awards Program at the end of our winter programs. The event was held at the City Hall Council Chambers on 3rd Street for the first couple of years. Mayor Rick Meehan would announce about 150 kids' names, and each recipient would receive their sportsmanship certificate. The program was later moved to Northside Park. The format was changed so there was more room for parents. The mayor signed a proclamation declaring February (and later March) as "Sportsmanship Month in Ocean City."

To my surprise, in 2019 the recognition ceremony was renamed the *Al "Hondo" Handy Sportsmanship Awards*. I am so honored because I was a strong advocate for good sportsmanship for many years. In fact, along with several other recreation professionals from around the state, for three years I testified at the State House in Annapolis, Maryland to try to convince the Maryland State House of Delegates and Senate Representatives to designate one month as Sportsmanship Month in Maryland. We were unsuccessful for three years.

In 2020, with the help of Director Susan Petito, we were able to get Governor Larry Hogan to sign a proclamation designating March as *Good Sportsmanship Month* in Maryland. I was so delighted when Susan asked me to assist with the announcement at the 2020 Maryland Recreation & Parks Association Awards Meeting. Governor Hogan also signed the proclamation for 2021 and 2022.

CHAPTER 49

THE *PLAY IT SAFE PROJECT*

Can you imagine inviting graduating high school seniors from around the state and the nation to your town, then providing them with free activities for three weeks? Well, that's exactly what had happened each year in Ocean City, Maryland, and it's been happening since 1989.

The *Play It Safe Project*, a statewide initiative that was held in Ocean City, Maryland was a unique program for graduating high school seniors. It's considered a model for resort towns. Although due to COVID, it hasn't been held since 2019, for over 30 years, it had been a main attraction for graduating high school seniors.

In the past, when the high school seniors came to town, they tended to bring with them many problems—from too much partying to too many vehicles on the streets. Year-round citizen didn't exactly look forward to their annual visit, but things changed with *Play It Safe*.

Here's some background on the program: In 1989, then Maryland Governor William Donald Schafer asked Ocean City Mayor Roland Powell to set up a committee to fight the abuse of alcohol and other drugs in our community. From this request was born the Ocean City Drug and Alcohol Abuse Prevention Committee—OCDAAPC—a group that worked in partnership with state and local government agencies, designated businesses, and concerned citizens.

I was asked to attend a committee meeting as a listen-and-learn opportunity. When your director calls you into his office, you follow his instructions and go to the meeting. The first person I recognized was Donna Greenwood, who eventually became the chair for the Ocean City Drug and Alcohol Abuse Prevention Committee. I had known Ms. Greenwood for several years through recreation programs. She greeted me warmly and asked if I was there for my director; I shared that I was there on his behalf to learn more about OCDAAPC and *Play It Safe*.

The committee's key responsibility was to implement the *Play It Safe Project*. Its mission: to encourage high school graduates to make informed, healthy choices while having responsible fun without the use of alcohol and other drugs. At the time of my meeting, two or three activities had been held. Ms. Greenwood asked,

> *Hondo do you think you could come up with few other events?*
> *I am not sure, but I will check.*

I was excited to get the meeting notes to my director as soon as I could. I informed him that the committee needed new events for student participants.

> My director said, *Well, what activities are you going to recommend?*
> *I thought I was supposed to give you the information for you to figure that out.*
> *If you are supposed to come up with some events, you need to get working on it.*

Wow! I had just been given more responsibilities; that day, I became a part of the Ocean City Drug and Alcohol Abuse Prevention Committee. Initially, *Play It Safe* was to be a one-week event in June. Upon joining the committee, I noticed graduates were still here after that week. I questioned why the project was not offered for a longer period, as all seniors don't graduate the same day or the same week.

One reason *Play It Safe* was only a week was its cost; another was the lack of volunteers. Our committee decided to seek more donations and sponsorships, and to recruit more volunteers. In response, the program grew over the years from one week to three weeks, with nearly sixty free events to honor thousands of recent graduates traveling to Ocean City for fun in the sun. How many are we talking about? Well, for example, 13,185 graduates attended in 2008 and 8,318 graduates participated in 2014. Graduates came from sixteen states, some as far away as Texas, and from Washington D.C. That number has changed each year.

For many years, the graduates were provided with free weekly rides on our city buses.

They just needed to flash their *Play It Safe* wristband. In addition, the graduates received t-shirts, pizza, and water at most events.

To make a long story short, I was involved with the program for 30 years. Donna Greenwood was the chair of the Ocean City Drug and Alcohol Abuse Prevention Committee. I became the vice-chair. We provided events such as Karaoke on the Beach with D.J. Donnie Berkey and beach dancing; Game World mini-golf and arcades were very popular. Trimper's Rides provided rides on their giant roller coaster. 48th Street Watersports offered paddleboarding, kayak races, and canoe races. There was a miniature golf tournament at Nick's Maui Golf. The 3-on-3 basketball tournament was held inside at Northside. Old Pro Golf had indoor and outdoor miniature golf late into the night. The beach volleyball tournament featured teams from many high schools. A pizza eating contest was held at Pizza Tugos. Dances were sponsored by The Original Greene Turtle. Laser Tag was held at Planet Maze and Game World. Tie-dye t-shirt designing was created at the Art League of Ocean City. The 61st Street Tennis Center supervised tennis tournaments. Jolly Rogers opened Splash Mountain Water Park and go-cart rides. Grand Prix Amusement batting cage time was offered. Indoor six-person dodgeball was held at Northside Park. Ocean Lanes Moonlight Bowling filled quickly. Some 300 businesses, organizations, and individuals contributed money and prizes. Volunteers provided more than 1,000 hours of service to the project. I called the volunteers who helped the high school graduates *Seniors Helping Seniors* since many of the volunteers were over sixty years old.

Working with the Worcester County Health Department and the Governor's Office, we were able to get 75,000 informative *Play It Safe* booklets distributed each year. DVDs were sent to each high school that detailed the *Play It Safe* activities and demonstrated what happens if the visiting graduates break the law.

This was a fantastic program that helped over 100,000 graduates from all over the country. I believe crime went down during the weeks of *Play It Safe*. This was one of my favorite projects to be involved in. Our committee believes we made it safe for the graduates. We believe that we saved lives and that *Play It Safe* made parents feel safe about sending their kids to Ocean City.

The program won the Maryland Recreation & Parks Innovative Programming Award in 2005 and the Video Showcase Award 2006. The program also received national attention when my article *How I Did It: Playing It Safe in Ocean City, MD: An Innovative Program for Vacationing High School Seniors* was published in the National Recreation & Parks Publication, Volume 43, No. 11, November 2008.

The website, developed by Bill Wheatley of Wheatley Computers BW Cyber Marketing, kept participants informed about the Play It Safe mission all year long. A statewide high school t-shirt design contest was held each year to raise awareness about the project.

In 2020 and 2021 the *Play It Safe Project was cancelled due to* COVID. Donna Greenwood issued a statement in the spring of 2022, formally bringing the program to an end and thanking all involved over its decades-of long history.

CHAPTER 50

GLOBAL GEAR DRIVE—FIRST IN THE NATION

Collecting sports equipment to be shipped to underprivileged countries was an enormous undertaking. Imagine seeing kids kicking a ball made of bundles of tape. Now think about those kids having a real soccer ball with your name on it. I was so intrigued about the idea.

Fred Engh, Founder and CEO of National Alliance for Youth Sports (NAYS) said, *How would you like to serve as the Global Gear Coordinator?* Of course, I said yes! When I was named the Official Global Gear Drive Coordinator for the Certified Youth Sports Administrators by NAYS, it was an honor. I want to thank Fred for the opportunity to serve. In my role, I oversaw Global Gear Drive collection efforts among CYSAs across the country.

At our NAYS International Youth Sports Congress in Denver, we kicked off the campaign. I asked CYSAs to bring any sporting equipment they could carry on the airplane. For example, they might bring a deflated football, basketball, or soccer ball. I encouraged them to bring equipment with their logo on it. I also coordinated a collection at the NAYS International Youth Sports Congress in Washington, D.C. Equipment came in from across the country. I received a picture of a kid in Zambia, I believe, holding one of those soccer balls.

The Global Gear Drive was created in memory of Sammy Wilkinson, an Ocean City boy who tragically lost his life at Northside Park. Sammy was the grandson of Fred Engh. The Sammy Wilkinson Memorial World Fund was created as part of the National Alliance for Youth Sports' worldwide initiative to lend a hand to countries in need around the world—countries that were unable to provide quality sports programs to children.

Sammy participated in several programs at the Ocean City Recreation & Parks Department. He had this smile I will always remember. He may not be here anymore, but he will always be near and dear to my heart. When I think of Sammy, it still puts a smile on my face.

Our area schools would be the first schools in the nation to participate in Global Gear Drive. New and used sports equipment was collected by students and shipped to underprivileged countries. Area school employees such as Stephen Decatur teacher Laurie Chetelat, Stephen Decatur Middle School teacher James O'Halloran, Berlin Intermediate School teacher Susan Johnson, Showell Elementary School teacher Becky Johnson, Ocean City Elementary School teacher Tracey Drocella, and Most Blessed Sacrament teacher Kim Allison all assisted with equipment drives.

This was one of my most rewarding experiences while serving as a board member of the National Alliance for Youth Sports and a Certified Youth Sports Administrator.

CHAPTER 51

HOSTING LITTLE LEAGUE ALL-STAR GAME OCEAN CITY V SALISBURY

You would think being selected for an All-Star team would mean something to all the players. You would think having a chance to represent your city would take precedence over other activities—even riding the waves. But not on this day.

Ocean City is a 10-mile barrier island, with the ocean and the beach being the main attraction. I knew it was a surfing city because I grew up in the area. This was on full display during a Little League All-Star Game in which Ocean City was hosting a team from Salisbury. The parks division crew leader, Ron Rickards, put the American flags up. His crew cleaned the dugout. He made sure the loudspeakers worked. The field looked good after being prepared for the game. I made sure the National Anthem was ready to go. The scorebooks, the scorekeeper, and umpires were available.

The home team is supposed to warm up first on the field. However, when it came time for Ocean City's team to warm up, there weren't enough players, so I had to ask Salisbury to warm up first. This was a little embarrassing. I was busy doing the parking lot stare, which meant waiting for the rest of our team to show up. It was a sunny, hot, "beach weather" kind of day. I couldn't help but think about what the waves must have look like. Anyway, the time was ticking down and the game was about to start.

The Salisbury Coach asked, *Will your team be taking the field?*

I answered, *No, we will be ready for the start of the game.*

Well—by game time, we weren't ready. We had to borrow a few players from Salisbury to play. We didn't have enough players even though it was a home game. We were forced to forfeit the game. We decided to play a pickup game.

It was about the third inning when four of my players came running across the parking lot. Some had their game pants on. Others wore their uniform shirt. They all needed some part of the uniform to be fully dressed.

When they arrived, I asked, *Where were you guys? We had to forfeit the game!*

They said, *Coach, the waves were banging…we couldn't resist!*

I should have known that most players on our team were surfers. When it came to making a choice between being on the hot baseball field or being in the breaking waves, they chose the waves. On that day, I learned what the waves of the ocean and sunny skies meant to the kids who lived in Ocean City.

CHAPTER 52

MEETING CAL RIPKEN

Meeting Hall of Famer Cal Ripken, Jr. was very special in and of itself. But not many people in Ocean City knew that he played in our Over 30 Men's Basketball Tournament. That's right! We got to see him play basketball for three or four years. Each year, he would bring a team down from the Aberdeen area to compete. The only thing he asked our department was that we didn't advertise he was playing—so we didn't. Members of the teams that played against him didn't tell other people either. He just wanted to play the games, then relax at his place in Delaware. No press was contacted. At the end of the tournament, they all wished they had known. I was able to get a few pictures with Cal. He is a good basketball player.

I talked to Cal Ripken Baseball about bringing summer baseball camps to Northside Park. He never actually came down. However, I was able to bring the Cal Ripken Baseball Camp to Ocean City for several years.

I did get to hear Cal speak on youth sports and good sportsmanship at the National Alliance for Youth Sports Congress in Orlando with four hundred of my colleagues.

CHAPTER 53

HONORED AS OCEAN CITY BECOMES AN ALL-AMERICA CITY

There are honors and there are honors. I considered being asked to serve on a committee to represent Ocean City, the city I worked in, to be quite an honor. In 2000, cities and counties across the nation were vying for the designation of the National Civic League *All-America City*. Our committee's goal was that Ocean City would win this award. The award recognizes the work of communities using inclusive civic engagement to address critical issues. The first award was given in 1949.

Along with Donna Greenwood, I was asked to serve by Chairperson Kathy Mathias, the wife of then Ocean City Mayor, Jim Mathias. It was such an honor, but I knew it was going to take up a lot of my time. I informed my supervisors; I got the go-ahead as long as I could still perform my other duties at work.

A committee of *who's whos* was assembled, and representatives throughout the city came together. Several hours-long thought-provoking meetings spanning over a year yielded a game plan that included input from everyone. At the completion of our meetings, three projects were nominated. Presenters would have to justify why Ocean City should be a finalist for the award.

The *Play It Safe Project* (described in Chapter Forty-nine) to benefit both visiting high school seniors and Ocean City high school graduates was one of the three nominated projects. The project played such a pivotal role in bringing the community together. Many city departments, businesses, and residents were happy to be involved. The other two projects were the Children's House by the Sea and the Coastal Bays Program. After a promotional event to inform the community, our application was submitted.

To our surprise, after a few weeks we learned that we were selected as an *All-America City* finalist. I was so excited, as was everyone else on the committee. Twenty communities were vying for the designation of *All-America City* in Louisville, Kentucky. Our fundraising efforts allowed our members and delegations to fly to Kentucky. Louisville showed their appreciation with *All-America City* flags hanging on light poles and decals on their sidewalks. Horns blowing, flags waving, cheering, singing, and music playing highlighted the day's events in the reception room. On the first day, each finalist committee conducted a presentation to reflect how their city worked together on their projects. Our delegation was a small one compared to some of the larger cities which had as many as 200 delegates.

Being selected as a finalist out of all the cities and counties in the nation in 2000 made us proud. The top ten finalists would become *All-America Cities*. We sat on pins and needles as the announcements began. One city at a time was called, but Ocean City did not make the Top 10. As joyous as the event was, the thrill quickly came to a halt. All our hopes came tumbling down when we were not selected. Many of us heartbroken, sadness set in as we left Louisville. But our leader Kathy Mathias got us refocused. She and Beth Gismondi of Gismondi Insurance Associates found out what we needed to do better. We reviewed our notes and resubmitted our application.

The wait was on to see if we would become a finalist again. Excitement ran through our committee when we learned that we were selected to the Top 20. This time, we were invited to Atlanta, Georgia for the finals.

We practiced our presentation and routine repeatedly. This time, we took the award-winning Stephen Decatur High School Choir to help with our presentation. This brought our delegation to over fifty participants. Flying to Atlanta, we hoped our dreams would come true. We had one final practice in the basement of our hotel the night before the ceremony. The convention room looked like a national political convention with all the delegation members of the Top 20 cities. Again, there were flags, signs, banners, and hats. Many members were dressed alike and in the same colors, representing their cities. We wore our Ocean City t-shirts and waved our OC flags and banners.

After our presentation, we had to wait until everyone else completed their routines. We were so nervous as the 2001 selection announcements began. The cities were announced in this order: Santa Clara, California; Delray Beach, Florida; South Miami, Florida; Fort Dodge, Iowa; Howard County, Maryland; and then—Ocean City, Maryland! Our team exploded! Cheering, hugging, crying, taking photos, jumping up and down. It was unbelievable! I called work to let them know about the designation—and they already knew. A press release had already gone out nationwide. It had been announced on our local television station within minutes of the selection. Everyone in Ocean City had also been waiting for the results. Our entire population was so proud. It was the best feeling that I had ever while working for Ocean City. To top it off, I had the opportunity to celebrate with students from Stephen Decatur—my former high school!

The feeling I had that night in Atlanta always comes back when I pass City Hall. When I remember the time we brought home that award, I still get chills all over my body. When I see those *All-America City* emblems on the front doors of City Hall, that sense of pride comes rushing back. When Ocean City was announced as an *All-America City* in Atlanta, it was so thrilling. After suffering a devastating defeat, victory was so much sweeter. I've learned this throughout a career focused on sports: *Victory is always sweeter after first tasting defeat.*

CHAPTER 54

THE ANNUAL TURKEY BOWL

When I was in college, one of my friends invited me to Cambridge, Maryland for Thanksgiving. He said, *I want to share something with you that my community does every Thanksgiving.* Their Annual Turkey Football Bowl was a tradition. This meant all the former football players would return home to play in this game—before eating their Thanksgiving meal. When we arrived at the field, there were cars everywhere along with three ambulances and a couple police cars.

I asked my friend, *Why are there so many ambulances?*
Because they play tackle with no equipment. There are usually lots of injuries. Today there will probably be a couple of broken arms, knee injuries, and twisted ankles.

I couldn't believe all the people who came to watch. It looked like a college football game with fans shouting the entire time. Players running full speed and colliding…it was hard for me to watch. I cringed each time there was contact.

I decided that I would like to do a Turkey Bowl, but I thought I would organize a basketball game instead. It seemed a lot safer. When I started working at the Ocean City Recreation & Parks Department, I started my own Turkey Bowl. I invited my friends from Bishop. We started with two teams: Over 20 and Under 20. We hooped it up from 9:00 a.m. to noon. We would then go home, clean up, and visit each of our mother's houses for dinner. Take me, for example: I wouldn't eat at home first. I would visit up to six of my friends' houses. One mother would fix me a small plate, and then I would be on to the next house. Our mothers were great, and a fun time was had by all.

The Annual Turkey Bowl was held for over twenty-five years. The teams started to expand over the years as the kids in the community started to get older. We ended with eight teams, with players ranging from 18 to 50 years old. Once the "Over 50" players couldn't get the younger teams to give points to make the games even, we stopped. No…I think we stopped because my team got too old. I am proud to say we only had one ambulance call in over twenty years. We now play Turkey Bowl Golf. It's not only more fun; it's much safer.

CHAPTER 55

EXCITEMENT AT THE CELEBRITY GOLF TOURNAMENTS

Taking about creating a buzz in Ocean City for the sports enthusiast— Celebrity Golf did that! Never would I ever see so many pro athletes at the same time. It was hard to believe. Director Tom Perlozzo organized "talk of the town" golf events in the early 2000s. Not long after that, he convinced the Town of Ocean City to build the Eagle's Landing Golf Course. One of the highlights of my career was to be a part of those Celebrity Golf Tournaments. These events became known as the best golf tournaments in the area.

Now I have met a few famous people over the years, but usually not all in one place. This was different. Year after year, these athletes would return for the golf outing. There were not only professional athletes— some were Hall of Famers. One was the Orioles player Dick Hall. Other professional athletes in attendance were Curt Shilling and John Kruk of the Philadelphia Phillies; Ken Griffey Sr. of the Cincinnati Reds; Scott McGregor, Tim Nordbrook, Ken Singleton, Elrod Hendricks, Tippy Martinez, and Sam Perlozzo of the Baltimore Orioles; Sam Jones of the Boston Celtics; Tom Matte, Toni Linhard, and Howard Stevens of the Baltimore Colts; Bill Robinson of the New York Yankees; Marshall Cropper of the Washington Redskins/Pittsburgh Steelers; Mario Lemieux of the Pittsburgh Penguins; Harold Baines of the Chicago White Sox/Baltimore Orioles; Dave Johnson of the Washington Nationals; and Bobby McAvan of the Baltimore Blast, just to name a few.

We also held a televised golf event that featured some big names such as Mike Schmidt of the Philadelphia Phillies, Johnny Bench of the Cincinnati Reds, and John Elway of the Denver Broncos. I have so many signatures on baseballs! It's hard to see the names clear.

CHAPTER 56
LEFT-HANDED BATTER
& THE CUP STORY

During my Little League coaching days, I worked with many players with many different talents. One day, I was talking to the kids in the dugout and didn't notice our batter at the plate. The umpire called time out and signaled me to home plate.

> *We have a problem.*
> I asked him what it was.
> *Your batter is facing me while he's in the batter's box.*

My player, with the bat on his shoulder, was facing the catcher and the umpire.

> I said, *You're left-handed, so you belong in the other batter's box. Step in the other box.*
> He said, *Thanks coach, I have a problem with that sometimes.*

As I walked away, I heard the umpire call me back. My player had stepped in the left-hander's batter box. He had switched hands and was still facing the catcher and umpire. I didn't leave the plate until I had him facing the pitcher. Ahhh, the things you see in Little League…

The cup story is actually from one of my players, Jay Yilmaz. It's about me giving instructions to the team. As the coach, I thought I had made myself clear on what was needed. Maybe not…

Coach told our team at the first or second practice that we each needed a cup. He kind of gestured to his groin. Of course he was talking about an athletic support to protect our future generations of baseball players. But I did not know that at the time, having a father who was not a sports guy. I was stumped, and I was definitely not going to ask my teammates due to the risk of being embarrassed. So, for the rest of practice, I pondered and imagined why we needed a cup… especially in the groin area. By the end of practice, I had the problem solved, though I was still a bit perplexed about the mechanics of the whole thing. After practice I mentioned to Mom that we needed to get a cup to put in our pants. It was so we wouldn't have to leave the field to use the bathroom! Needless to say, she smiled and informed me of what we really needed to get, which was a bit of a relief!

CHAPTER 57

MARYLAND TERP BASKETBALL COACH LEFTY DRIESELL

One Saturday morning, I stopped in the office to pick up something, hoping to get in and out before anyone could see me. The office and gym were closed. As soon as I put the key in the door, a group of six kids from the neighborhood came running across the parking lot. They started shouting.

Hondo! Can we shoot basketball?
I am only going to be here for about five minutes.
Of course they responded, *Well, can we shoot for five minutes, please?*
Okay, you can play. Five minutes.

I then got them a basketball.

Just as I was ready to walk into the gym to get the kids, I heard a knock. Then there was another knock at the front door. I just knew someone else wanted to play— I was sure. I looked up and it was *Lefty Driesell,* former head coach for the Maryland Terps.

Hondo, can my son Chuck and I shoot around for a few minutes?
Sure! Come in.

I sent them down to the court opposite of where the kids were shooting. I thought this would be a great opportunity for the kids. It was a chance to meet a former basketball coach from the University of Maryland. So I called the kids over, and they gave the basketball to me.

Would you guys like to get some autographs from the Maryland Terps basketball coach? He is down at the other court.

They looked at each other and one spoke up: *Hondo—give us the ball back; we don't have much time left.*

What was the lesson learned? *Some things that might be important to you aren't so important to others.*

CHAPTER 58
I LOCKED MY KEYS IN THE OFFICE

Susan Petito and I seemed to be the last to leave work most nights. We both loved our jobs and were very dedicated. We were always preparing for the next day—trying to get that one last task done before we went home.

One night, I was there by myself. I remember suddenly realizing that I had to get home. I grabbed my stuff and headed out. As the front door was closing, I realized I had left my car keys on my desk. I tried to reach for the door handle—but it too late. I had a jacket, but it was in my car. And *this* just happened to be a very chilly night. It was one of the coldest nights of the year.

There was a telephone outside our office; however, I didn't have any money. This was in the early '90s, and we didn't have cell phones back then. I decided to go across the street to a local restaurant to ask if I could make a call. I tried to reach my wife, but there was no answer. It was about 9:00 p.m., so I guess she was sleeping.

I decided to walk back to the office. Once I got there, I realized I could call home collect, so I did and, again, my wife didn't answer. I kept trying to call her, and on the third attempt she answered.

Hello, this is Al.
She said, *What?* and then hung up.

I called her collect again, and I told her what had happened. She instructed me to call someone who worked with me and hung up. The

194

fifth time I called, she argued with me. I could tell she must have fallen back to sleep. She then shouted, *Okay! Let me get dressed!* I waited in the cold for about thirty minutes and decided to call collect one more time. She answered.

> I said, *I thought you were getting dressed.*
> *I'm still sleepy; I am on my way.*
> *Thank you; I will be waiting.*

Meanwhile, it wasn't getting any warmer. There were city vehicles left in the parking lot each day. Each vehicle was supposed to be locked. It was so cold that I decided to check to see if, by luck, any vehicle was left open by mistake. I checked all the vehicles and the very last one was open—thank God! I took a seat inside to avoid the wind and cold. By now, I was shaking from being so cold. Once I got warmer, I dozed off. I woke up suddenly and jumped out of the car, but no one was around. I got back inside and dozed off again. The next time I woke up, there was a car leaving our parking lot. I jumped out and raced to the next stop sign, where the car was headed. I realized it was my wife's car. Just as she was leaving the stop sign, I hit the back of the car. She hit the brakes. I called out her name and opened the door. She said, *You're lucky! I didn't see you, so I was going home.* I *was* lucky because I knew she would have left me.

Lesson learned? *Make sure you have your keys before you leave work.* Funny—after that incident, it was something I always asked at the end of my workday: *Where are my keys?*

CHAPTER 59

MY NIECE TAKES ME TO THE MOVIES

Although my niece was only one year old at the time, our first cheerleading routine at my father's house sealed our relationship for life. We have been close ever since. I don't think our connection will ever change. I became that uncle who could always get her to stop crying; the uncle who took her to every amusement and attraction in Ocean City, Maryland. I could see the smile on Brianna's face whenever she would visit. The dollars just came pouring out my pockets like magic as we moved from place to place. Besides me spending lots of money whenever I have been with Brianna, we have always had a fantastic relationship.

Every two weeks, my brother James would pick her up for the weekend. She would call me as soon as she got in his truck. She would always say the same thing: *I'm here. What are we going to do?*

I spoiled her each Saturday she was in town. We ventured to Pizza Tugos to eat some pizza and play ping-pong; Old Pro Golf to play indoor and outdoor miniature golf; Dumser's Dairyland for ice cream; Nick's Mini Golf for—well, more miniature golf; outdoor tennis in Berlin; lunch at her favorite places; Eagle's Landing Golf Course for a putting contest; the boardwalk for a long stroll—and much more.

I spent all kinds of money on her. I told her I was going to give her an invoice when she got old enough to pay me back. Jokingly, one weekend I said to her, *When are you going take me somewhere?*

My niece called me during that week. She said, *Uncle Hondo—I want to take you to the movies next weekend.* I was so surprised. She must have thought I really wanted her to take me somewhere. I agreed without thinking about how old she was. She was only six at the time. Had she spoken to her dad or her mom? I asked her what movie we were going to see.

She said, *Wreck-It Ralph.*
Ask your father where the movie is playing.

He told her *Wreck-It Ralph* was playing Saturday in Salisbury at 6:30 p.m. I said to myself, *Oh no, I have to work indoor soccer all day, then go to a movie that night.* I wasn't going to be home all day, which was not good.

The next Friday she called and asked, *Are we still going to the movies tomorrow?*
Yes, but ask your dad again where the movie is playing.
She did and told me. *It is now playing in Ocean City at 4:15 p.m.*
I thought, *Great; I could go to the matinee and get home early.*
I said *We got a date. See you tomorrow!*

The next day at Saturday soccer, I made arrangements to leave work early. *My niece is taking me to the movies,* I shared. About 3:30 p.m. my niece came racing into Northside Park, right through all the hundreds of soccer players.

She jumped into my arms and asked, *Am I still taking you to the movies?*
Yes, but where is your dad?
He is outside, but he is tired.

I got my things together and went outside to my brother's truck. I told him to follow me to the movies, about ten blocks from work. When we got there, my niece came walking over to me with her car seat. I then looked up and saw that my brother was leaving.

Where is your dad going?
Home because he is tired.

I strapped her car seat in my back seat. I couldn't believe my brother just left. We started walking towards the movies.

Your dad must have given you a lot of money for our movie, right?
No.
You were supposed to be taking me to the movies.
The movies are right there. She pointed to the theater.
That's when I knew my brother had gotten me again. We got to the ticket booth, and I said,
One adult and one child for Wreck-It Ralph.
The cashier said, *$16.*
What? How much is it for an adult?
$8. (I knew I had him then; he had made a mistake.)
Well, how much is it for a six-year-old kid?
$8.
Are you kidding me?
My niece said, *Uncle Hondo, you always have to pay for the movies.*
I answered, *Yes, you're right.*
As soon as we went through the doors, she said,
I'm hungry.
As we walked towards the concession stand, she shouted, *I want that one—the Wreck-It Ralph snack.* It was made up like the McDonalds Happy Meal.
I asked, *How much is that?*
The concessions clerk said, *$6.50.*

I had to get some popcorn and a drink: another $7.00. I was now out $29.50 for a movie I thought my brother was paying for.

We finally got into the movie, and she started talking about the movie. When the movie started, she continued telling me about *Wreck-It Ralph*. I had to tell her to be quiet, but she was so excited I couldn't stop her. She looked me right in the eyes. I did my best to keep my eyes on the movie. I was tired myself. I started to doze off.

A few minutes later, she said, *I need to go to the restroom.*
I said, *Okay.*

I was thinking I could get a quick nap. Then, I remembered she was just six. I jumped up to follow her out to the restroom, so I thought. She started going towards the concessions. *I want some candy.* I bought her some candy and got some myself: another $10.00. She started back into the theater. I asked her if she still had to go to the restroom. She said, *Oh yeah.*

We finally got back into our seats and enjoyed the rest of the movie. As we came out of the movie, she started to rub her stomach. I asked,

Oh no! What's wrong?
I am hungry.
What?
Yes, and there is a McDonald's right down the street.

Of course, I stopped at McDonald's. After we ordered, she told me to go find a seat and she would bring the food. As we left McDonald's, she asked if she could get ice cream at Dumser's. Of course we stopped, and both of us got ice cream. While we were eating our ice cream, my brother called and wanted to know where we were. I told him we were on our way and thanked him for taking me to the movies.

Lesson learned? *Be careful what you wish for. Kids are smart. So are brothers.*

CHAPTER 60

GOOD THINGS HAPPEN TO THOSE WHO DON'T QUIT

The best advice I can give to any young kid would be not to quit on your dreams. Set your goals in life; but remember goals can change—and that's okay. The first goals you choose to reach your dreams may not work out. But they're *your* dreams, so don't quit on them. Don't give up on them. My goals changed all the time because of different circumstances, but I never quit on my dreams.

During high school, I wanted to be a professional soccer player. When I graduated from high school, I wanted to be a high school basketball coach. When I went to college, I wanted to be a physical education teacher and a coach. While at college, my goal changed to wanting to be a professional baseball player. However, because of an injury *that* goal changed. When I became a recreation professional, I wanted to make the biggest impact I could on our customers.

I wanted to be a professional soccer player because I didn't think size mattered that much. I would dream about playing soccer for a career. Once I made the starting lineup for my high school, I thought it was possible. When I was awarded the Most Valuable Player Award during my senior year, I was convinced I could make soccer a career. I wasn't able to put in the necessary work in college to advance my goal, though.

I also wanted to be a high school basketball coach. I wanted to follow in the footsteps of my high school and college coach, Ward Lambert. I did get a chance to be a coach in high school at the junior varsity level. I also assisted with the varsity team. I was not employed by the county education system, so financially things didn't work out for me. At least I reached my goal of coaching—although for only one year.

My next goal of playing professional baseball was dashed after playing a successful summer league season. Upon returning to college for my senior year, on the first day back I broke my patella (my kneecap). My first collegiate coaching opportunity came following my college graduation. I was asked to assist my college baseball coach, Deane Deshon. I enjoyed coaching that season, and I learned a lot from Coach Deshon.

Once I became a recreation specialist, I decided that I was going to be the best recreation professional I could be. I was dedicated to the profession for years and advanced to a recreation programmer.

I applied for a supervisory position but didn't get the job. I was saddened because I felt I deserved it. I was faced with a choice of leaving and seeking other employment or staying and remaining dedicated to my work. I decided to stay after a conversation with my mother. She convinced me not to quit and purchased a plaque for me to hang in my office to remind me every day of that important message. The plaque read *Don't Quit.* I looked at it every day when I opened the door to my office.

Years later, I received a position that I wanted: recreation manager. Along the way, I received many accolades. Receiving the "Citizen of the Year" award twice has to be among my proudest memories, especially since this award came from the community, the Ocean City Chamber of Commerce, and the Ocean City Elks Lodge. I am so glad I listened to Mom and didn't quit. I am so proud to have my name displayed on a plaque in City Hall on 3rd Street.

Some of the other Citizen of the Year winners listed on the plaque were very prominent people: Arthur T. Davis; JD Quillin, III; Thelma

Connor; Dr. Francis Townsend, Jr.; William Greenwood; Louise Gulyas; Dorothy Henley; Dan Harris, III; Adam L. Showell; Norman Cathell; Donna Greenwood; Granville Trimper; India Bandorick; Wayne Cannon; Pam Stansell; Brice and Shirley Phillips; Kathrine Panco; Kathy Mathias; Macky Stansell; Dawn Hodges; Lou Taylor; and Michelle Fager.

CHAPTER 61
COMMENTS FROM THE COMMUNITY

I asked a few people I came to know during my career if there was anything they would like to share about me.

JIM MATHIAS, FORMER SENATOR FOR MARYLAND, FORMER MAYOR OF OCEAN CITY

From the first time I met Hondo, what I will always remember is his smile and positive attitude. They have always been contagious! His friends, co-workers, and children he has coached and mentored throughout their lives all agree.

He continues to wear that natural smile and exhibit his positive "can do" attitude. We, as residents of Ocean City, Maryland, the Eastern Shore, and the entire state have always been the beneficiaries.

In addition to successfully growing state and nationally recognized recreation programs in the department, what Hondo really built was solid foundations for thousands of kids who are now mature adults and mentors for their children and the youths in their communities. This will always be Hondo's legacy! We thank you, Hondo, and are eternally grateful to you.

SUSAN PETITO, OCEAN CITY RECREATION & PARKS DIRECTOR

Having spent over thirty years of late nights in the office with my dear friend and colleague, Albin "Hondo" Handy, I can attest that he is a loyal and dedicated individual. He is one of the most caring people I have ever had the pleasure of knowing, and I feel I can now beam like a proud parent as I had the distinct pleasure of being part of his support team, cheering him to victory as his well-earned career accolades piled up.

I watched him grow from a raw athletic talent to a seasoned recreation veteran, sharing his wisdom of sport and sportsmanship with both the youths and adults of our community. From the moment I met him, he shined as a team player in the workplace, and I watched as he radiated enthusiasm and goodness in all his interactions.

He has an infectious smile, a happy chuckle, a fun sense of humor, and a charisma about him that endears him to everyone he meets. His impact in the community, through his Recreation & Parks efforts, may forever be unmatched, and the stories he's collected over his many years in the field, I can only imagine, could fill a thousand books.

GERALD GROVES, FORMER OCEAN CITY RECREATION & PARKS DIRECTOR

I had the privilege to serve as director of Ocean City Department of Recreation & Parks from 1978 to 1984. During this period, Al "Hondo" Handy joined our efforts in providing services in support of opportunities for all age groups and abilities.

He brought experience and history of successful participation in sports and understood the importance of well-maintained facilities and coaching fundamentals. Hondo embraced these qualities in providing services but first had to self-evaluate and commit to excellence in his approach to his personal life.

The result was a remarkable sharing of vision, skills, creating life values through activities, and touching the lives of thousands of youths in the Ocean City community over thirty-nine years. His recognition and honors over the years were earned, but his legacy is the lives he touched through his work. He remains one of the most remarkable individuals to serve Ocean City.

SCOTT DAVIDOFF, DEPUTY CITY MANAGER, CITY OF CLERMONT, FLORIDA

Al changed my life—plain and simple. When I was a kid, he was an icon to me and all of us. What we saw was an adult we respected who was always interested in not just our athletic achievements, but in who we were as people. His positivity and kindness were always so infectious that a ragtag group of kids put him on a pedestal which, at that time, had no place for adults outside of our sports idols.

When I decided to make Parks & Recreation my major in college, my parents asked what I would actually be doing. When I told them I was going to be like Hondo, they understood. During my career I have always strived to have the impact on others that he had on me.

My son and daughter have been lucky enough to meet Al when we have come back to Ocean City to visit; they've heard many stories about him. I heard he was finally retiring, and we were talking about it at the dinner table. My son said, "I am glad you got to meet your hero." Al really is a hero to a generation of Ocean City Parks & Rec kids.

ANDRE FOREMAN, ALL-TIME LEADING SCORER IN DIVISION III BASKETBALL HISTORY

Hondo has meant so much to me in ways that a lot of people (including him) might have never known, but now they will. Let's start at the beginning: The first basketball league I ever played in was started by Hondo, along with sidekick Greg. We even got shirts, which was big back then. I think I played on the Berlin Hardware Lakers or maybe Dennis Trucking, I forget. That was the start of me playing organized basketball.

I ended up following Hondo's footsteps and went on to play basketball at Salisbury University. Throughout those college years, I managed to come back and help out with the basketball camps Hondo ran in OC. Once I graduated and started playing overseas, I often came home and helped with Hondo's Play It Safe Project. It was always great for Hondo to keep me in mind, so I could help give back to the community and share my time and my stories.

One of my proudest moments is when Hondo was able to get one of my autographed jerseys displayed at the local Applebee's. He has done so much for me; I will always appreciate how special he is and how giving he is. He is truly one of the great ones and a blessing for our small Berlin family. Thanks, Hondo, for all you have done for me and my family. Oh, yeah —thank you for introducing me to golf. I am a work in progress on that one.

BOOK EXCERPT SUBMITTED BY MARY BETH CAROZZA

These observations are shared by Senator Mary Beth Carozza, who represents Ocean City in the Maryland State Senate. Mary Beth is a long-time family friend who has seen Al "Hondo" Handy in action in his coaching and leadership roles over the years and who has worked with him in elevating good sportsmanship in the state of Maryland.

Al "Hondo" Handy has had a tremendous impact on our local Shore community and, on a personal note, on my family over the years. His passion for good sportsmanship is having a lasting impact in Maryland.

My sisters and brother grew up playing sports in the various Ocean City Parks & Recreation leagues, and Hondo was always there for us. Whether it was the encouraging word, the look to straighten us up, or just a hearty laugh when we did something funny on the field or the court, Hondo was our rock.

With Hondo, it wasn't about the win/loss record but more about putting the team before himself. Good Sportsmanship was never just a motto for Hondo. He lived and exuded it, and his enthusiasm prompted so many young people, parents, and coaches to be part of something bigger than themselves.

With all the egos involved in sports, Hondo never made it about himself. He was constantly recommending others for awards and other recognition. This included my own brother-in-law, Jeff Wootten, whom Hondo nominated for National Coach of the Year Award, in 2003. Jeff received a prominent award because of that nomination.

Toward the end of his successful run as a leader at Ocean City Parks & Recreation, Hondo took his local program to the state level when he asked me to introduce legislation designating a Good Sportsmanship Month in Maryland. He was a popular witness in the Maryland General Assembly, and his tenacity and good nature paid off when Governor Larry Hogan designated March as Good Sportsmanship Month in 2020.

When Hondo retired after thirty-nine years with the Ocean City Parks & Recreation Department, it truly was a highlight of mine to present him with one of my first Maryland State Senate citations recognizing his heartfelt commitment to serving youths and families throughout our community and the state of Maryland.

CHAPTER 62

HONDO'S RETIREMENT CELEBRATION/FUNDRAISER

I have to admit that my retirement celebration/fundraiser was one of the most amazing events I have ever been a part of. Given the short amount of time that was available to pull the event off, the people in our area showed how wonderful they are. My mother had cancer and that affected me every day. Several of my co-workers have had cancer, and so have many of my friends. So, I decided early that when I retired, I was going to do something to benefit cancer treatment and research. The timing of my retirement was perfect. The John H. "Jack" Burbage, Jr. Regional Cancer Care Center had recently been constructed on the campus of Atlantic General Hospital, near my home. I mentioned the thought to my friend Tammy Patrick, development officer at Atlantic General Hospital at the time. We next met with Toni Keiser, vice president of public relations at Atlantic General Hospital to pitch the idea. We talked about the possibility of my retirement event benefitting the cancer center. I told them I had spoken with several people who would be willing to help.

We decided to set up a meeting. I put together an outstanding event committee which included Tammy Consigli, then of Coastal Style Magazine; Dawne Pappas and Dawn Hodge of The Original Greene Turtle; Melanie Pursel, then executive director at Greater Ocean City Chamber of Commerce; Kim Kinsey, Kate Gaddis, and Susan Petito of the Ocean City Recreation & Parks Department; Carol Everhardt, president and chief executive officer of Rehoboth Chamber of Commerce, and of course Tammy Patrick and Toni Keiser. We discussed promotion, who to invite, the cost, the food, the setup, and the check-in at the event. I informed them that the event would be held at Seacrets. Leighton Moore, my classmate and owner of Seacrets, and his wife, Rebecca, had given me their blessing to host the event there.

Atlantic General Hospital Foundation's promotion of the event on social media was tremendous. There were also articles in the Coastal Style Magazine by Alison (Clary) Pappas; The Daily Times by Sara Swann; Ocean City Today by Morgan Pilz; The Dispatch by Shawn Soper; and the Stephen Decatur Hawk newsletter by Kaitlyn Mourlas, editor-in-chief. There was even a segment on WBOC Delmarvalife.com hosted by Lisa Byrant and Jimmy Hoppa. My retirement photos were taken by professional photographer Grant Gursky.

The weekend of my retirement celebration/fundraiser started with a complimentary hotel stay at The Residence Inn by Marriott, and my room featured a gorgeous view that overlooked the bay.

When I arrived the night of the event, I couldn't believe how beautifully Morley Hall was decorated. Large sports balloons, along with soccer candy, basketball candy, and baseball candy were everywhere. The community was very generous in providing donations to ensure the night was a success. Flowers by Alison donated flowers, Sweet Disposition donated the cake, and Wockenfuss Candies donated the candy. My good friend and one of my coaches, DJ Tuff, donated his DJ services.

There was a large display of my favorite sports photos with some of the girls' basketball league players. There was a display table with handouts about my career in Ocean City and the Coastal Style Magazine article on my retirement. There was another display of proclamations from Governor Hogan, Senator Carozza, and the Worcester County Commissioners. I had already received a proclamation from the Town of Ocean City, Mayor, and City Council and a Key to the City presented by Mayor Rick Meehan.

More than two hundred fifty of my friends attended the event, which far exceeded what we had originally imagined. Present and former recreation & parks directors attending included Gerald Groves, Tom Perlozzo, and Susan Petito. Members of my State Championship basketball team including Oliver Purnell, Ron Dixon, Fason Purnell, Alfred Harrison, Larry Waples, Larry Duffy, and my golf partner Pat Henry were also there. Representatives from Atlantic General Hospital Foundation and the John H. "Jack" Burbage, Jr. Regional Cancer Care Center were Michael Franklin, Toni Keiser, Tammy Patrick, Greg Shockley, Todd Ferrante, Jack Burbage, and Virginia Pappas. Head Salisbury University football coach Sherwood Woods and Vicky Jackson Stanley, Mayor of Cambridge, Maryland, Attorney Pete Wimbrow, and Michael Guerrieri attended the celebration. My friend Greg Purnell spoke about our history working together starting at City Hall. Many of my family members attended as well as many of my coaches from Recreation & Parks; business owners and members of community organizations were also present along with many more friends.

It was a great retirement for me, and my friends helped raise $7,695 for the Cancer Care Center. It was a very successful event.

MY RETIREMENT SPEECH BY SUSAN PETITO

Al Handy began his career with the Ocean City Recreation & Parks Department in 1980, and he has held positions as a public grounds specialist, recreation specialist, recreation supervisor, and recreation manager over his illustrious thirty-nine-year career. He has proven to be an inspiration and mentor to thousands of children over his tenure with the Town of Ocean City, but his reach goes way beyond our area, as many of his efforts have been felt globally.

Al Handy has been involved with the Ocean City Drug and Alcohol Committee for nearly thirty years, serving a portion of that time as vice chair. He has worked with the Play It Safe committee since its inception, and proved to be an invaluable team member, guiding volunteers and leading activities.

He initiated the program's volleyball, basketball, and dodgeball programs, and has supported the effort to keep thousands of visiting high school students safe and positively active when in Ocean City.

As the smiling face of the Recreation & Parks Department, Hondo actively sought to attend the meetings of most town civic groups, educating their members on the value of youth involvement in positive recreational endeavors, and engaging the already philanthropic-minded memberships in expanded philanthropic endeavors specific to Ocean City's youths. He has served as a member of the Optimist Club and has been very active with events sponsored by the Elks Lodge #2645, having been recognized with the Elks' Citizenship Award as well as its Citizen of the Year Award.

Hondo served on the advisory board for the National Alliance of Youth Sports and worked with them to establish a National Certified Youth Sports Kids program. He was the vice president of the Salisbury University (SU) Maroon and Gold Club and has continuously served in that capacity for the last ten years. He has also been a member of the SU Board of Visitors. He served ten years as a sports columnist for the Oceana Magazine, covering local recreation activities and area sports. He published an article in a national publication on the Play It Safe Project in Ocean City and was instrumental in securing Ocean City's first "Tree City USA" award.

Over his career, Hondo has received many awards, among them the Best Youth Organization Director by Coastal Style Magazine, an honor bestowed upon him by the voting public; the Ocean City Citizen of the Year, a prestigious recognition awarded by the Ocean City Chamber of Commerce; and the Maryland Recreation & Parks Association's Citation Award, given each year to a recreation professional who has demonstrated significant and exemplary service in the field of Parks & Recreation. He received the Worcester County Drug and Alcohol Abuse Council Award and the Task Force Award; a citation from Governor Martin O'Malley for his receipt of the MRPA Citation Award; the Maryland Recreation & Parks Association Video Showcase Award; a citation from Governor Robert Ehrlich for Citizenry; he *was part of the team that received a citation from Governor Paris Glendening for the All-America City Committee; a citation from Governor Larry Hogan for 39 years of distinguished and outstanding service and the Maryland Recreation & Parks Association Innovative Program Award for Play It Safe, among others.*

Along the way, Hondo has had the opportunity to meet celebrities like Magic Johnson; Muggsy Bogues; Dale Curry; Art Shell; Sam Perlozzo; Michael Steele; Brenda Frese; Gary Williams; Mark Turgeon; Hulk Hogan, John Elway, Harold Baines, Emmitt Smith, Tim Brown, Dick Vital, Bill Walton, Tony Banks, Herschel Walker; Lonnie Baxter; Johnnie Damon; Dickie Vitale; Pat LaFontaine, and Cal Ripken. He hopes to finish writing the two books that he's been working on for a few years, do some traveling, and play some golf, along with spending more time with his wife, Regina, and his niece, Brianna.

CHAPTER 63

THANK YOU, OCEAN CITY, MARYLAND!

All things considered, I am happy I picked up that little orange ball. I am even happier to have had the opportunity to start my life over as a young man. I will always be grateful for my time working in Ocean City and for the Ocean City, Maryland Recreation & Parks Department. The professional training and education I received by attending conferences were amazing. Having the opportunity to be a member of professional organizations such as the Maryland Recreation & Parks Association, the National Recreation & Parks Association, and the National Alliance for Youth Sports has been one of the highlights of my career. I have been able to travel all over the country to network with other professionals and bring information and education back to Ocean City. My co-workers were a team, and we got things done as a team.

The Mayor and City Council saw the impact and positive influence our department programming provided for the residents and our visitors. I will miss the interactions with the participants, especially the thousands of youths. My experience in Ocean City will always be cherished; after all, this was the place where my career started and ended. I want to thank the community for all you have done for me, and the department—for being like a family. Sportsmanship is what I would like to be remembered for, because it was the number one thing that I tried to promote for the department.

Having the sportsmanship ceremony renamed the 'Al "Hondo" Handy Sportsmanship Counts Awards' will keep me smiling for the rest of my life.

My recreation job started on January 3, 1980. I continued to learn about recreation & parks until the day I retired. In fact, I was still on my computer when my wife came to pick me up on my last day of employment. Ocean City has been good to me. I hope I have been good for the department. Leaving a place that was my second home for nearly forty years wasn't easy. But, reflecting on my decision, it was the best time in my life to say goodbye. Thank you, Ocean City!

CHAPTER 64

IN CLOSING

FRIDAY, MARCH 29, 2019—MY LAST DAY

As I raced out the door for the last time as a recreation manager for the Town of Ocean City, I was full of joy and excitement. I had finally made it! Most of my friends from our department were there to say goodbye. Also, one of my dearest friends and past president of our Teen Council, Jeff Gisriel, and his kids were there representing his entire family. But, when I saw the face of Kim Kinsey, my dear friend, I wanted to cry—not because I was sad about retiring, but because I was leaving her. You see, we had worked together in programs for so long that neither of us probably thought this day would ever come. But I held back my tears because I didn't want to upset her any more than I already had. We were extremely close and always will be. I just did what I always do; I broke out with a smile that I hope none of my co-workers will ever forget. After a group photo by Ocean City Today, I jumped in the limo that my wife had waiting for me. My associates encouraged me to open the sunroof of the limo and wave goodbye to the place I called home for thirty-nine years and three months.

I wanted the staff and Ocean City to know that I gave it all I could each and every day. I worked up to the last minute of my retirement. I was still working when my wife arrived to pick me up. Our office manager, Norma Simmons, had to tell me my wife was there. I finally finished—I rushed out so fast that I left my jacket in my office!

Was I happy to be leaving? No. Was I sad to be leaving? No. I came to realize that it was time for me to go. After all, the other members who I started my career with, those I called the "4Ever Four," Greg Purnell, Ron Rickards, and Calvin Ginnavan, had already retired. I had planned my retirement, down to the month, for many years. I will always love my time working in Ocean City and will continue to be a No. 1 promoter of our department.

No more late-night work at the job with our director, Susan Petito. No more being the last two employees to leave. No more having to secure the building. No more long drives to work each day. No more budgets to be responsible for. No more approving of purchase orders. No more work orders for our Parks Division. No more recruiting and training employees, coaches, and other volunteers. No more requesting sponsorships and donations. No more speeches and attending community organization meetings. No more educational trainings to attend. No more playing weatherman for our outdoor programs. No more being responsible for concessions, with Donna Davis, for weekend sporting tournaments. No more coaches' meetings. No more adult league meetings. No more official's contracts. No more approving of league schedules. No more social media complaints. No more Play It Safe events for the high school graduates. No more late and sleepy drives home— just a few thoughts that ran through my head the night before my retirement.

As we drove away, I didn't want to look back. I wanted to end that chapter of my life and begin focusing on my next chapter. At that moment my wife, Regina, said, *"Job well done."*

If I had any doubts that Friday, March 29, 2019, was the right day, it was all confirmed minutes after the limo driver dropped us off at Dover Downs. Within twenty minutes, we had won $3,200. I quickly called the office and spoke to Kate Gaddis, sharing my good news. She responded, *Isn't retirement great?!*

I didn't want to go back to the Ocean City Recreation Department until I was good and adjusted with my retirement. I already have to go back each year to attend the youth sportsmanship awards, the *Al "Hondo" Handy Sportsmanship Awards.* I now had the opportunity to write the book about my life growing up on the Eastern Shore of Maryland, my feelings about being one of the first African Americans to integrate Worcester County Schools, winning a state basketball championship, my journey to college, the role sports played in my life, what led to my return to the place I called home, and finally a career that some say may not ever be matched in Ocean City. My cousin Larry wanted me to name the book *The Little Boy from Bishop.* I had so many titles running through my head, but one kept coming back time after time: *Defying Expectations* by Al "Hondo" Handy.

SERIES OF WBOC TV DELMARVALIFE APPEARANCES

http://www.delmarvalife.com/delmarvalife/whats-happening-june-27-2017/
June 27, 2017

Summer Camps Memories
June 25, 2018

Stephen Decatur State Basketball Championship 50 Year Celebration
January 27, 2020

Checking in with Al "Hondo" Handy
August 24, 2020

Hondo Handy's Podcast
September 1, 2020

SPECIAL THANKS TO:

Thanks to Mary Lib Morgan for all your hard work editing my book. After meeting with you, I was convinced that you were the person I wanted to review my book. Thanks for all the phone conversations and for believing in me. You went above and beyond to help make my dream come true.

Allison Clary Pappas, Author of *Old Dogs, New Chapters* for her editing of my first proof.

Fred Engh, Best-Selling Author of *Why Johnnie Hates Sports, Match Sticks, Never the Twain Shall Meet* and *You Gotta Be Kidding Me!* for his professional encouragement, suggestions, and thoughts.

Jeff Thaler and Ned McIntosh, Author of *The Baffled Parent's Guide To Coaching Indoor Youth Soccer* for inspiring me and featuring on the front cover.